HOW TO BUILD A PEOPLE'S ARMY

MOVEMENT

Kalonji Changa

HOW TO BUILD A PEOPLE'S ARMY

RATHSI
P U B L I S H I N G

ISBN: 978-1-936937-09-7

Cover Design: Tafari Melisizwe
Back Cover Photo: Sheree Swann

CONCRETE BLUES (Word/Sound/Power) 3⁹

BACK TO BASICS
Class Struggle u⁷
* Encountering other organizations or troops
* Organizational Courtesy
* Criticism and Self-Criticism (Lessons from Mao)

A SNITCH IS A GLITCH IN THE MATRIX 50
(Word/Sound/Power) Courtesy of StaHHr

LOOSE LIPS SINK SHIPS 51
* How to organize "Operation Cop Block" in your area

SOUNDING THE AKOBEN 54
* Ascension to Soul Rhapsody
* From Rage City to Serving the People
* Black is Back
* Hip Hop University
* Hip Hop Politricks
* Hip Hop as a tool to organize the community

PRESENT DATE IN TIME (Word/Sound/Power) 71
Courtesy of Eboni Joy

THE OBAMA-NATION ABOMINATION 73

COINTELPRO: The Destruction of a Movement 77
* The Palmer Raids
* NOW-INTELPRO
* The Assassination of Tupac Shakur
* The San Francisco 8
* Cyber Snitches, Internet Informants and Tele-terrorist
BANG ON DA' SYSTEM (Word/Sound/Power) 87
Courtesy of Imhotep Kushan

Foreword

Looking at the state of the so-called struggle for liberation today, it's hard to believe that five decades have passed since such notable stands as, Brown vs. Board of Education, Bus Boycotts or the deep south sit ins. We have come so far and yet here we sit wondering at the next move. It seems we have been stuck in neutral for many years now while every lurch forward stalls the momentum and causes world wide regrouping. As we watch thousands die globally on a daily basis, survival and entertainment dominate the agenda of most. This far down the line, the feeling is that everyone knows the way and simply need encouragement.

They don't!! Too many have grown into their 20's and 30's without the P.E. classes and educational rallies that were so prominent between 30 and 40 years ago. We created a vacuum spanning a time when we could not afford to relax and ride the laurels of past deeds. During that vacuum, America built bigger prisons and put into effect the king Alfred plan that most do not believe exists. Roughly thirty years ago California had 11 state prisons and approximately 19,000 inmates. As of 2009, inmates in California prisons total nearly 200,000.

During the same period, the so-called cold war ended and America's secret agents flooded back home highly trained and motivated with nothing to do. In no time government of the people had given them a new target, the people.

Technology went ballistic finding new ways to spy on you the unsuspecting public without leaving the slightest clue. While we pondered what would be the most revolutionary path forward and bickered amongst ourselves, oppression, already institutionalized quietly planted the seeds of our destruction on a global scale. Behavior modification and control through atmospheric

7

spraying, tampering with food sources and water was given the highest priority. The sensory deprivation units in this countries prisons and clandestine clinics known as Security Housing Units serve to break the spirit totally both physically and mentally and also to create Manchurian candidate types for insertion back into our communities. While you are a 24/7 occupation for the terror we call government, you have not kept pace with the systematic sophisticated increases designed to make you disappear. Here we sit!!!

In California, 2009 brought with it proposition 9 called the victim's bill of rights. The first and most prominent part of this proposition concerned the rights of victims to know when those who had victimized them were to be released from prison or went to board for review. The last part which had no bearing on the rights of victims, gave the prison board the power by law to deny parole dates to inmates in the SHU programs from 5, 10 or 15 years at a time without explanation. You simply go before the board now and they tell you to come back in 15 years and you have no legal remedy. It does not matter that you have been in prison for 45 years already, it's the law.

The institutional politic of warehousing people because their social awareness and political outlook cause them to advocate on behalf of those oppressed masses where ever the may be found on the planet has now become a slow motion death sentence. Although America is quite adept at the practice of singling out and persecuting those individuals who stand and resist, it is a worldwide epidemic that reaches into the lives of the less fortunate all over the planet.

With laws like proposition 9, three strikes and many others in recent times, the powers that be are establishing the modern doctrine for world domination. We cannot assume that what is prepared in this kitchen is merely for local consumption because we are the first to experience it.

We must come together on the universal nature of this beast and make people understand the need to stand against oppression in any form, anywhere.

The policy of our demise is woven into the fabric of this society and mandates the way we die in the streets at the hands of the boys in blue. We must discard the notion that there are rouge police outside the jurisdiction of their precincts who kill us at their own whim. The policy dictates our designation, puts that bullseye on our backs when we are born and sets us up for incarceration or death in the streets by quota. There is no such thing as a bad cop, a prison guard who is out of line with procedure or any committee or board simply consumed with power, the whole structure is rouge.

In all this there is the underlying socio-political, economic structure that determines who, when, where and how many must die or be pressed into positions of increased servitude to maintain the true desires of the few that rule absolutely. In any given situation flesh and blood will take on and magnify or diminish the attributes of those they serve. A police officer may seem to be one of the most quiet spoken and caring people around while he may have a polar opposite who behaves like a pit bull at all times. He is still a police officer following the policy set forth by those who run this country and he will kill you when it is his time to do so. He does not try to find out whether or not you are a bad guy and therefore deserving of death. He is on duty and his duty is to follow policy, and policy is you die.

Until we understand that our rage must be directed at the masters and not the slaves. We will not continue to expend our energies in useless marches and focus groups. The people will continue to be the victims of that overflow of misdirected anger and in the way of policy's unleashed response. Some of us have learned this and much more, but for most there has been no progressive education in terms of the adversary's true agenda and how we should relate to it.

That lonesome feeling of standing in the middle of the road wondering why no one is with you is not an isolated feeling. It is experienced over and over by many who believe the necessities of the struggle are known to many more than actually have a clue. Remembering where we have been is vital because in that legacy these lessons are played out on a grand stage bloodied and brutal while in the same period heart warming and inspirational.

We cannot forget the times gone where explanations the people seek now were driven home on the backs and lives of those who chose to willingly resist and those who standing idly unbelieving were struck down by the very same juggernaut of policy. We must look to a future where oppression, pain and suffering administered by brain dead drones wearing the masks of slave breakers, plantation overseers and executioners is not a waking nightmare. Most importantly we must focus on now where we live and breathe and create and die.

While so many wander aimlessly connected to nothing, desiring nothing and believing in their hearts there is no point outside the routine, we sadly must begin again. What has been instilled in us by circumstance and the fact of our existence is the basis for the lesson plan. It is the example we must use to reopen the survival schools in greater number in every community so that awareness, understanding, preparedness and commitment becomes the culture we live and grow within.

Some few are already in the streets in communities across the country feeding the people one on one out of a strong personal commitment to make things said in the warmth of living rooms, things done in the cold and desolate abandonment of the streets. Others who understand the need must join them and those who simply know their own need to give of themselves. The agents who wait in the shadows to disconnect us one from the other by distorting history, look just like us and multiply daily. There are many who wish this history was not ours but was one more thing that could be rewritten to glorify them and all those like them who clamor for greatness at the expense of the people they claim to serve. Those of us who suffered through some of this history have never been burdened with the desire to shine like stars and confound the people with our brightness. The fact that we have not shouted from the highest mountain our tales of woe and past deeds has left a vacuum some of our more needy and unimaginative folks feel they have the right to fill in any manner they see fit.

COINTELPRO is still with us in truth and deed. Tactics tried and true are swirling amongst us pitting one against the other as always. People still believe that when the police say it is so it must be based in fact. The establishments that bind and oppress all of us are the masters of falsehood and manipulation, innuendo and supposition. Knowing this we still allow sugar coated fabrications to undermine every step we take progressively forward.

When we speak of passing on the torch, there must be a foundation upon which the torch can be sustained otherwise the flame is lost forever. No ideal is snatched from the wind by force. It is instilled precisely in fertile soil to bring forth a generation more steadfast than the last.

Know us for who we are as well as who we were. Honor us for what we stand for now as in times harsh and unforgiving. Acknowledge and fortify the principles we have chosen to live by that don't bend in the wind like trees. Honor yourselves by letting go of the false flags and political doctrines that simply enhance the façade while leaving the heart to rot and fester hidden from those who seek the true path to liberation.

In all of this the difference between a rebellion and a rally will become clear and the people will not be left holding the proverbial bag.

Shaka At-thinnin
Black August Organizing Committee

Introduction
Blessed Are Those Who Struggle

"Blessed are those who struggle, oppression is worse than the grave; it is better to die for a noble cause, than to live and die a slave"-The Last Poets

At first glance at the title of this book, many may assume that it is another manuscript based on war and violence or something dealing with some form of outdated militancy. Why do I say that? I say that only because when most people heard I was writing a book, they would ask me what was the title and then when I would respond, the look on their faces would tell it all. The look would say to me, "here he go with that Black Power shit"...When I would give them a synopsis of the book the usual response would be, "oh okay, we need that".

I wrote this book because at this point in history there is an awful lot of bullshit being put out and passed off as being a reflection of revolutionary culture.

Before a baby walks he starts off by scooting, crawling and then eventually the baby walks. We have some folks that think you can just come out of the womb and start running. I think it is time that we take it back to basics. In this so-called modern world of advanced technology people are allowed to do what they feel, say what they feel, hide behind a screen name and violate any codes that they feel without even the slightest thought of any type of repercussions or consequences. Why? Because there are absolutely no rules and there is no accountability.

You don't have to be whom you say you are to be respected as such, all you have to do is look good on the Internet and dress the part. For centuries our people have sacrificed everything so that we could continue to exist. And now anyone can speak on whatever they would like even if they have no knowledge of the subject. Just look the part and act like you might know.

I learned that the weak, unprepared, "wannabe's" truly out number the authentic, loyal and disciplined. A comrade used to say, "Some people can't tell the difference between a poet and a revolutionary". Nothing against poets, there are certainly some dynamite, inspirational poets, that I would consider revolutionary. The Last Poets, The Late Great Gil Scot-Heron, Mutabaruka, Amir Sulaiman, Sunni Patterson and many others would definitely make up the soundtrack for revolution. They are certainly some of the boldest and flyest that have done it. My point is that there are some folks that get pumped off the fan fare; regurgitating some shit they hardly understood themselves. Since the masses are blind some self-appointed experts become "Mr. or Ms. Revolutionary". All of a sudden you have someone who has not made an effort to make change within his or her self, let alone the community and he or she becomes an "authority" on the liberation struggle. But who am I to judge, if the people like it, I love it. I will that the efforts I make as a comrade, father, brother, and son can be of some type of benefit to the people as a whole.

Writing a book was not on my to-do list, I would much rather had saved that task for the "scholars". And I am certainly not a scholar. Nothing wrong with the scholars, we need scholars. As long as what it is they are teaching is practical. We need scholars, but we also need balance. All the theory is real cool, but theory without practice is nothing. To quote Huey P. Newton, Co-founder of the Black Panther Party, "A picture is worth a thousand words-don't watch what I say, watch what I do, I can talk all day, but action is supreme". Our people talk a good game; we can make anything sound good. I guess that's why we are the progenitors of rap, because we are the best rappers. We as a people have become so accustomed to talk- that we think that's all that has to be done. So with some nice sounding words and some cool sound bites, the preacher, the politician and the so-called Black leadership (which is usually a combination of a preacher and a politician) can talk that money right up out of your pockets. Then the preacher will tell you that "money is the root to all evil" (but he will beg you for yours); the politician wants you to put money into his campaign and the so-called black leadership wants you to "support the cause". At the end the results are the same. They get rich, you stay poor and our situation as a whole gets worse. Meanwhile, we remain a respect-lacking race of people. We don't get respect primarily because we don't respect ourselves. Not only do we not respect ourselves, we don't respect our babies, our youth, our peers, or our elders. We talk about respecting our elders however our actions prove different. An example of not respecting our elders would be the situation with Dr. Yosef Ben-Jochannan. Dr. Ben (which he is more commonly referred to) for all practical purposes is a living legend and Pan Afrikan icon that should be afforded the same respect that any revered scholar of his caliber would get in any other arena. Folks like Dr. Ben, Cheik Anta Diop, Theophile Obenga, Dr. Frances Cress Welsing, Marimba Ani, Dr. Bobby E. Wright and others helped to shape shift Pan Afrikan thought on this continent and abroad. So they cannot be forgotten nor can they be disrespected. As the Great Ancestor Dr. John Henrick Clarke pointed out, "there was no such thing as a nursing home In Afrika", we took care of our elders. It is ironic that Dr. Clarke's good friend and Comrade, Dr. Ben the noble son of Afrika ends up inside of a nursing home in Coop-City in the Bronx, New York. Someone told me he was put there "for his own safety". That is totally unacceptable. We talk about the pyramids we built, the fact that we were the architects of civilization and you mean to tell me that we cannot develop an Afikan-centered facility to take care of our own? Not preparing a place for our own, contradicts all the talk we do in regards to being an Afrikan. Dr. Ben's consistent commitment to outwardly opposing European domination and falsehood should be commended. His contribution to countless authors, educators, scholars etc., must not go unnoticed. We as a collective have failed our youth, and now we are failing our elders as we have failed our Ancestors. But I guess, that is what is to be expected of an able bodied people who won't have the decency to fight for their own comrades who fought tooth and nail for them. Not only that it is pure selfishness to live your life and not be concerned about those who came before you nor those who are to come after you. The countless Brothers and Sisters who have been kidnapped and held behind enemy lines who are being punished as prisoners of war and political prisoners. Brothers and Sisters who put us on their backs, risked their freedom and some who have literally given their very lives. Comrades like Imam Jamil Al-Amin (H. Rap Brown), Hugo "Yogi" Pinnell, Sekou Odinga, Jalil Muntaqim, Marshal Eddie Conway, The Move 9 and others currently held captive. Many who are being tortured and abused to this very day, not in Guantanamo Bay, but in Pelican Bay, not in Angola Africa, but in Angola, Louisiana, and not on some foreign island but on Rikers Island, Colorado Supermax and many other modern day institutionalized slave dungeons. While some of us sit back and do nothing, not a damn thing. How will you explain to tomorrow's children why you sat back and ignored the cries and screams of your comrades, your brothers, your sisters as you walked around with invisible blind folds and earplugs? "See no evil, hear no evil". Will you cop a plea of convenient amnesia or will you submit your manhood to this system of global White supremacy/Black annihilation, because "we got a black president". We got a black president –reminds me of El Hajj Malik Shabazz when he spoke about the house nigga saying, "What's the matter boss we sick". Brothers and Sisters we have to do more than study, we have to do more than research and more importantly we have to do more than talk. We have to listen, plan, plot, strategize and be prepared to spring into action at the right time. Oftentimes when we get to the part about action, some hopelessly devoted lost soul comes along and attempts to make efforts to discredit or discount what we are saying. Well I'm here to tell you that the days of selling wolf tickets are over. We ain't selling wolf tickets and we certainly are not buying any. Jermaine Jackson (Michael's brother) had a song out back in the day called "Let's get serious", I think time is way overdue and we must get serious. We must constantly train to fight and we will be victorious beyond the shadow of a doubt. In the words of Deputy Chairman Fred Hampton of the Black Panther Party, "Dare 2 Struggle, Dare 2 Win and if you don't Dare 2 Struggle, then goddamnit you don't deserve to win!

FROM WHENCE THEY CAME

My peoples' 1st eye so blind, I speak to 'em in Braille.
I've been persecuted so long; I'm too experienced for hell.

Over qualified, lost in the abyss of my own mind.
The Creators design, crucified by my own kind

My ruthless acoustics render cultural cowards useless,
My renegade guerilla repertoire leaves idiotic synthetic
rebels toothless-
They're fruitless.

The words I speak are so dope, a heroin addict couldn't
shoot this.
So I chop it raw, let it seep in ya' mental pores,
Travel through ya' corridors-to awaken all you warriors.

I ride or die, investigate my genetic code-
a walking time bomb
On pigs and snitches, programmed to explode.

A runaway slave, I shook my shackles loose-
190 proof, my intoxicated truth is bulletproof.

The mic's my accomplice; she's rude I'm obnoxious.
We hold the crowd hostage with though provoking topics,
That shines like fiber optics.

With no remorse, I blow these capitalist pigs off course.
With brute force, return they ass to the source,
From whence they came.

FAMILY 1ST

"We are not a problem people; we are a people with problems. We have historic strengths; we have survived because of family. The Black Family of the future will foster our liberation, enhance our self-esteem, and shape our ideas and goals"- Dorothy Height

Everything that exists within the universe has an order and anything that doesn't have an order is chaotic (chaos). Whether we are dealing with reproduction, how we breathe, how we eat or how we walk there is an order as to how things work. Taking on the task of being a community organizer, a freedom fighter, a revolutionary or what have you is no different. You must organize yourself, your immediate family, your extended family and then the masses. You start with your house, your community, your city and on from there. At times it could be a very difficult task but with practice comes growth. Unfortunately, many of us have been taught and continue to teach to organize internationally when we can't handle the basics in our own homes (sort of like the U.S. trying to control affairs globally when its own house is on fire). There has to be an order. Don't get me wrong, I'm not saying we should be selfish and only be concerned with ourselves and live from a capitalistic state of mind. We certainly must labor to improve the whole and one of the best ways to do that is to maintain your home base. Imam Jamil Al-Amin formerly H. Rap Brown was fond of saying "If you can't beat yourself, you can't beat nobody else". Your family is your first cadre or unit that you should fight to keep in order-"By Any Means Necessary". Now, I know that some people will read that statement and make an attempt to use it as an out to escape working on behalf of the people, don't try it. I'm not suggesting you abandon the people, like the song goes "Worse comes to worse my people come first". But at

19

the same time don't abandon your family either as the old saying goes, "blood is thicker than water". Building towards our future is a full time labor of love and we have to make sure that our families love to be part of that labor and love to labor so that together, we can enjoy the fruits of that labor.

to some extent are neglecting our babies. Oftentimes we will be so caught up in the masses that we overlook those who truly love us, who are right in our faces. Its almost equivalent to sweeping the dirt out of one room of your house into another, you still have a dirty house. We venture out to fight on behalf of the people and in our minds we expect our wives, babies and other family to "understand the mission". Although our intentions may be wholesome, we are causing just as much harm to our societies, as we are good. The results are that our family suffers, our community suffers and our nation suffers. Our absence leaves our children not knowing us and oftentimes not even knowing themselves. We miss out on important developments and achievements in their lives. In some cases we are away from home so long that if and when we return we are like strangers. Some of our greatest have been guilty of this, sacrificing their families for the sake of the struggle for our liberation. Malcolm X was guilty of it, Martin Luther King was guilty of it, Amos Wilson, Imari Obadele and the list goes on…Not to compare myself to these great ancestors, but as an organizer, from an organizational perspective I must confess that, I am no exception; I too have been guilty of it. Amongst the few things I regret in life not being with my children as much as possible would rank in the top two. I have made a vow to spend the rest of my existence on this plane nurturing and educating my offspring as much as possible. We can no longer aid in the destruction of our nuclear family and at the same time say we are fighting "for the people". That is a serious contradiction. If everybody is fighting for the people and no one is taking care of the babies it's going to be impossible to solve the problems we face. This is a perpetual cycle that we must break. We know that there is already an issue with fathers being absent amongst the masses. Being a Black male in America is an issue in and of itself due to incarceration, murder and even grueling work hours for low wages just to get by. So it is imperative for those of us who know what time it is to be a moral rudder to guide Brothers in the right direction. Quite often by the man being absent, the woman is forced into the arms of the very system that you are supposed to be fighting against. They are forced to endure the humiliation, demoralization, and embarrassment of having to seek public assistance for food, clothing and shelter for our children. Oftentimes, they have to deal with the negro go between who works for the system that makes every effort to degrade and disrespect. They have to go through countless hours of twaddle just to get some funky ass breadcrumbs and some chump change that wouldn't satisfy a kid in a candy store. The thought of that alone should make the average man beat the brakes off of his own shoes and get in gear to turn that vehicle in the right direction. Aside from that, you should be ashamed and embarrassed to have this same "white man", lock you up, dictate and mandate you to support your children. This is unacceptable; we must do better than that. We will do better that, in order to be victorious.

Many of us come from homes with single mothers and in many cases single fathers. However, the unit is complete when there is a mother/father component to reinforce the foundation and strengthen the structure. Boys need their fathers to teach them how to be men and girls need their mothers to teach them how to be women. Children need both parents. It is my opinion that the absence of the father helps to destroy the moral fiber of a society. According to statistics, our children are more likely to experience poverty, depression, develop anti-social behavior and display traits of bad characteristics i.e., fighting, lying and cheating. There is an increased risk of drug and alcohol abuse, illiteracy, teen pregnancy, sexual abuse, rape and disease. They are left vulnerable as prey forced into an immoral lifestyle for mere survival or street credibility. These same children fall into "the trap" distributing plantation poison, prostitution, becoming abusive men and even homosexuality. Our daughters are being lured into strip clubs to "dance to advance", taking off their clothes in an effort to make ends meet. Parasitical pimps lurking around corners and alleys looking to make our daughters the next victim to be tricked into a real life tragic fantasy of hopelessness and despair created to suck the life out of a "damsel in distress". There strolls another angel gone astray. No hero to save the Black girl lost, that we helped to misplace. Every Brother that I converse with sings the same song, "That would never be my daughter". That sounds good in theory, but in practice every Sista on the ho' stroll is somebody's daughter.

We leave our sons in situations to sell drugs, rob and murder as a means of survival. They began to join apolitical, undisciplined street organizations for a family bond and a sense of belonging. Then the journey begins as they start acting out a self-destructive, self- hating reality that masquerades as crew love. A way of life that maintains, benefits, and secures an oppressive empire at our offspring's demise. Recruiting for these types of street organizations has always been a piece of cake because we as a people have forever had the desire to belong to something be it a club, fraternity, sorority, team, clique or what have you. That's something that is natural within our culture, so if there is no positive, strong group to be part of, then oftentimes our children turn to the opposite direction.

Of course that lifestyle ends up being a contradiction to the way of life that you profess to lead. Our children knowing that the cards society has dealt us has come from a loaded deck, oftentimes end up responding in a hostile and sometimes violent manner. We must protect our children in every sense of the word-physically, mentally and spiritually. We have to be there to guard their hollow parts from nonsense that aids in our ruin as a people. Especially our younger children, we must teach them who they are, who we are and also about our place of origin. It is our responsibility to educate them about how we got into this situation, why we are here and where we need to go. I know people in the so-called conscious community whose children can go into detail about who Drake, Lil Wayne and Nicki Minaj are but they don't have a clue as to who Marcus Garvey, Kwame Nkrumah or Fannie Lou Hamer was. How can we say we are working to save the babies, when we are allowing them to commit subtle suicide? Nonsensical music, television and trends must be eliminated from their cipher, if we are serious about their future. We have to make sure that our sons and our daughters have healthy diets, and are physically fit, able to protect themselves and their families. We have an obligation to reinstate rites of passage in our homes with our immediate family, our extended family and our comrades. No one's gonna save us but us…. Family 1st.

Family 1st.

23

A Few Things That You Can Do Today to Change Your Family's Reality:

- **Communicate with your children**-If for whatever reasons you absolutely cannot be there today call them. That phone call from you, just hearing your voice means more than you can imagine. Children love to talk, pay attention you will learn something.
- **Take them on outings**-Some of the fondest memories I have in regards to my father are just taking trips or even simple walks. You don't have to have a whole lot of money in most cities there are plenty of parks. I haven't met a child yet that doesn't dig the park or a regular old playground.
- **Give them positive affirmations**-Be sure to consistently shower the babies with positive affirmations. Positive affirmations aid in strengthening their self-esteem and also to build their character. It helps them to be more aware and focused which will carry them a long way.
- **Transform your "B M", or "Baby Mama" into a Queen**-I frequently hear Brothers complaining that the Mothers of their children aren't conscious. My response is simply you knew that when you first lay down with her. Granted in some cases you may have ventured into this bold new way of thinking after the fact, but we are still responsible for our actions and inactions. In some cases, Brothers want to change the game in the 9th inning, the Sister was used to certain standards (that you agreed with) and then all of a sudden you read a book and you want all the previous rules to go out the window. That's not how it works. If your relationship with your child's mother is irreparable, then at best you can treat her in as high regards and with as much respect as possible. Regardless of whatever she is or

whatever she's not, one thing is for certain is that she is the Mother of your child. On that alone out of respect for your child, she should be honored. Treat her like your B M and you will get those types of results. Respect her as a Queen Mother and she just may operate as such.

- **Respect Your Parents-**I have actually gotten into a couple physical altercations with dudes that yelled at and cursed their Mothers out in front of me, and these were so-called conscious folks. Even if you disagree with them as your parents they are due a certain level of respect.

- **Respect Your Family's Beliefs-**I see some brothers and sisters that get caught up in the whole religious debate issue. My position is what you eat don't make me shit. Whatever floats your boat. I am not going to spend my time arguing about religion. I can't say I respect my Elders and my Ancestors and I know for a fact that some of them were and still are Christians, but yet I spend my whole life bashing Christianity. My point is that if your family has certain gatherings, holidays or whatever, just because you don't celebrate or participate, doesn't mean you shouldn't attend. You should take every opportunity possible to spend time with your family. You don't have to believe as they believe just to fellowship. I know people who read 3 books and now all of a sudden everybody is savage but them, because they don't eat meat or celebrate holidays. Miss me with that shit! If you are privileged to have a family, you know that's one of the few things that are certain. Show your family love.

"It takes a village…"

The Afrikan Proverb, "It takes a village to raise a child", has been so over used and watered down that it has nearly been rendered impotent. On a certain level it has become a slick sound bite for applause from negroes that won't bust a concord grape in a fruit fight to crackers that want to prove that they are down with the people. It has become a vantage tool for folks seeking the popularity vote. In 1996, even crusty ass Hillary Rodham Clinton, who was First Lady of the United States at the time, took advantage of the proverb by naming her book, "It Takes a Village". That year the book became one of the #1 New York Times Bestsellers. While many Black folks in the US applauded Hillary for using an African Proverb and being married to their original "first black president", Bill Clinton, much of white America were appalled. She received immediate opposition, most notably from racist republican Bob Dole, who during his acceptance speech at the Republican National Convention that year, made the statement, "with all due respect, I am here to tell you, it does not take a village to raise a child. It takes a family to raise a child". In spite of Bobby Dole's two cents, in 1997, Hillary continued to pimp the title and received a Grammy Award for Best Spoken Word Album for her audio recording of the book. Of course no Afrikan child benefited off of the sales of any of these books or compact discs.

Building a People's Army off of the village concept

My point in addressing the aforementioned is simply to remind us that anyone can talk the talk, but how many are willing to walk the walk? Our goal here is to put theory into practice. In the last section, I talked about the importance of your family or our families in the building of a People's Army. In this next section I want to deal with the importance of **The Family** in the building of a People's Army. From this point on, when you see 'the family', note that I am making reference to an extended family, a family beyond an individual's lineage or household. The family is camaraderie on a higher level even beyond your basic comrades. The family is revolution without having to say revolution. It exists and to some extent moves in stealth like manner. It is the type of organization that does not have a name or at least it doesn't have a name that is broadcast to the masses, in fact the masses know nothing about it, sort of like the concept of the mob so to speak. We call that the "family ties principle". The family ties principle is the taking of the concept of family and bringing into fruition a close knit, clandestine cadre made of members that build together. The family bonds together mentally, spiritually, physically and economically. The family trains together as far as martial arts, on the shooting range, archery and other self-defense tactics. As an expanded unit beyond the individual households, the family works together as far as building an economic base, acquiring land, health and nutrition, political education, legal affairs, home schooling (or independent schools), institution and nation building. The family is built on a foundation of love, trust, loyalty, integrity, discipline, morals and ethics. The fact that it is not advertised or spoken about serves as a safety net against infiltrators. There is no open membership. Existing family members, screen potential family members through interactions at public affairs, programs, events and other gatherings. Potential family members come with recommendations and a track record that speaks for itself. It is a long-term process; there is no rush in building the family. The principles are quite similar to any other relationship, if you rush into the situation based on emotions rather than intelligence and sound right reasoning then the results could be disastrous. Family members treat each other, as a true family should with honor, placing each other in high regards. All of the children refer to each other as brothers, sisters or cousins and to the adults as Baba, Umi, Aunts or Uncles. If there is a special occasion, birth, naming ritual, wedding, graduation or any other ceremony, all of the family makes an effort to attend to show their love and support. At least once a month, different family members sponsor a family feast, dinner or potluck in which families discuss affairs and fellowship. Constant building and amity forges a cohesive bond that encourages and enables development and expansion amongst the comrades. I often hear folks refer to each other as comrades and family but they never invite each other to their homes and they are not familiar with each other's spouses or children. The reality is they are more acquaintances than family. You have to know thyself and also know those around you, particularly those who are considered your a-alikes. The beauty of organizing in this manner is that everyone knows each other, so there is a higher level of accountability and responsibility. Unlike your basic community organization, your role is much more up close and personal, so if you drop the ball it is clear and evident to the adherents.

A few ways to strengthen the family ties principle:

Communal living- Communalism serves several purposes. You have the opportunity to practice cooperative economics, responsibility and accountability (whether it is thru sharing of duties, which would include chores, bill payments etc.) Communal living is a sure way to know one another beyond the public image or persona.

Train together- As our Comrade Balogun Abegundee is fond of saying, "the mat is the truth." Training together thru exercise and workout routines, martial arts, on the range, archery, paintball and contact sports helps to build character, teamwork and it also encourages and aids in strengthening weaknesses as individuals and as a unit.

Study together- Oftentimes we find folks who invent every excuse in the world to avoid political education and group study. It is virtually impossible for one to advance as an organizer or a revolutionary without political education and group study. Especially in these days and times where we have such heavy low-intensity warfare being waged thru so-called "advanced forms of technology". Even on the battlefield Comrades like Che Guevara was so serious about political education classes that he wouldn't even allow his troops that missed classes to participate in certain activities. Show me a cadre that does not make a concerted effort to engage his/herself in regular group study and I will show you someone who is not serious about liberation.

Road trips- taking long distance trips together can reveal a lot about a person. It teaches about a person's level of patience, discipline, respect and values. In many cases after a nice long trip or two, the average comrade will have learned more about another than most previous encounters.

Remember that a family that lives together, trains together, studies together and plays together, will better function together. Peace to all those who do good!

14-Karat Garvey

Oftentimes, our people look at our existence as some type of "mystical magical" program, rather than endurance, intelligence, perseverance and sheer determination. Quoting the late great comedian Robin Harris, (when referring to a group of unruly children in which he called "Bebe's Kids") "We don't die, we multiply". It is no secret that our people have been downtrodden, exploited, demoralized and in many cases left totally devastated. So much so that when people speak of a recession it really doesn't even apply to many Afrikans in America because our financial grade has been consistently "in the red". In actuality, the only reason most Black People even started using the word recession is because that's what the powers that be whispered was going on. If the American government and their propaganda machine would have whispered that the economy was picturesque and that these were the best of times, then the underprivileged, downheartedly devoted multitudes would be humming to an identical tempo. There are no new remedies for old ailments. The answers have always and still exist; the seeker has to unearth the solution. The question that should be asked is who is willing to pursue the plan and put it into its proper perspective? The Hip Hop group Little Brother, in one of their songs posed the question, "Do you really wanna win or do you just wanna look good losing"? That is where our people are today and have been for quite some time. I grew up in the projects in Bridgeport, Connecticut, and like most inner city tenements a lot of us have or had our priorities jacked up. I remember back in the mid 80's, when crack was introduced in the height of "Reaganomics", in an effort to numb the pain of poverty many of us took on 'government jobs' as street pharmacists. We peddled crack, coke, dope and weed with hopes of getting rich while on the flipside further driving our neighbors and communities further into paucity and destitution. One of our fashion statements and means to broadcast our "success" was to purchase big gold cable rope chains with huge gold medallions on them. These chains ranged from $700 to about $5000. Then you had the leather bomber jacket, leather goose downs and sheepskin coats which ranged from $250-$450. BMW's, Audi 5000's, Broncos and the Mercedes Benz were the cars of choice in the hood. The purpose for taking this trip down memory lane is because all of the above mentioned material objects, along with some 3 or 4 finger 14k gold rings, were sported by some of the poorest of us, who desired to "look good". Here it was, we were dwelling in rat and roach infested conditions with the outside aroma of fresh pissy hallways, bloodstained syringes on the playgrounds and elevators that were stuck most of the time (which doubled as a public restroom for some), and our main concern was looking good. Many brothers and sisters lost their lives because of these materials, getting robbed and shot over some bullshit. Many received 45-plus years in the penitentiary for doing things to maintain the lifestyle. Shocking to many of us was finding out that this "gold" that we bought had absolutely no value. I remember going to a pawnshop to get some extra money to bail a friend out of jail and learning the hard way. I arrived with about $7,000 worth of jewelry and was laughed at by the owner of the pawnshop when I told him that I wanted to hock my gold to get some currency. We got into a heated argument when he asked me how much I paid the Asians for my gold-dipped aluminum. Still not convinced by that incident, I went to a reputable jewelry store and was told in a much nicer tone that the "gold" I owned depreciated the moment I walked out the store. At that moment I began to realize two things. The first was that the "valuable materials" in which we owned really had no value and secondly, that many people of other nationalities had absolutely no respect for us. The whole time I was gullible enough to believe that the Asians that I shopped with were cool, but the truth was that they were really playing a role in our exploitation and we were aiding in our own demise all in the name of being "fly". Fast forward to over a quarter of a century later, and Afrikans in America are still focused on style over substance while lacking power and respect.

When it comes to a blueprint for our survival, we really don't have to venture far back in history; master plans have been laid out clear and plain with many examples in the 20th Century alone. "The Father of the RBG", the Honorable Marcus Mosiah Garvey introduced Afrikans globally to the bold concept of "Africa for the Africans at home and abroad". Garvey came with a special blend of Pan Afrikan Nationhood, which included the Black Liberation flag that many of us still proudly fly today. Fashioned in 1920, by members of Garvey's organization the Universal Negro Improvement Association (UNIA), the red, black and green flag was created in response to a popular "coon song" penned by two racist crackers, J. Fred Helf and Will A. Heelan entitled "Every Race Has a Flag but the Coon". The song written in 1900 was a tremendously popular ditty in the U.S. and U.K. Marcus Garvey was quoted in the *Africa Times and Orient Review* as saying, "*Show me the race or the nation without a flag, and I will show you a race of people without any pride*". Being a proud nation of people a national flag was befitting. At a time when Black folks were being physically lynched wholesale, Garvey was on a mission to liberate the hearts and minds of our people. It is sometimes hard for some folks to fathom that it was nearly an entire century ago that this unsung leader of our people was able to maneuver and commandeer a defacto nation within a nation that would shape, mold and to a great extent serve as a litmus test for many prominent leaders for decades to

32

come. Notables such as Paul Robeson, Bob Marley, Elijah Muhammad, Malcolm X, Huey P. Newton and many others were directly influenced by the philosophies of Mr. Garvey. Even Harlem street legend Ellsworth "Bumpy" Johnson, was influenced by Marcus Garvey, often donating food and money to the poor in the community. The UNIA paved the way and laid a foundation for The Nation of Islam, The Black Panther Party and countless Black Churches and other institutions that have impacted and unified Afrikans on a global level. Without a doubt, the Honorable Marcus Mosiah Garvey and The mission of the UNIA is one of the reasons our organization, The FTP Movement came into fruition generations later.

With an understanding of a need to provide a voice for Afrikan people and to disseminate our own information, Garvey published a newspaper, the *Negro World*, which by 1920 was translated into 7 different languages and had a circulation of at least 200,000. With an early "Do for self" attitude, he knew that our nation had to be self sufficient, independent and self-reliant. Mr. Garvey contended that monetary attainment was the quickest and most effective way to achieve self-determination. It was with that mode of thinking that he developed the Black Star Line, a shipping business used for exchange and to transport passengers back to Africa. The Black Star Line sold individual shares of stock valued at $5 a piece in which the proceeds were used to secure three ships. He also established the Negro Factories Corporation in which he offered Afrikans the opportunity to purchase stock. The Negro Factories Corporation ran three grocery stores, two restaurants, several farms, printing plants, and a steam laundry to name a few. He also had his own military, The African Legion along with The Black Cross Nurses to aid in the people's well being. It is safe to say that during The Great Depression many Black People in America survived off of free food and services supplied by the UNIA. The lessons learned from the Honorable Marcus Mosiah Garvey stand as a symbol to our succeeding in this present era. The first lesson is that we should have an undying love for our people. The second lesson is we must have an unwavering declaration of loyalty and commitment. The third lesson would be that no individual has made an impact without an organization or a team. Although, Marcus Garvey was the spearhead of the operation, it was the rank and file members and supporters of The UNIA that provided a firm foundation and aided in the advancement of the movement. These are a few very important ingredients to a good recipe to victory.

You don't have to "struggle" to struggle

For some reason many of our people have convinced themselves that being part of "the struggle" means that you have to struggle financially. Nothing can be further from the truth. The first thing is the word struggle has to be eliminated from our vocabulary when it comes to our fight for self-determination. Secondly, one of the reasons many of our people are not getting involved in our efforts is because they don't want to be "poor, raggedy, and out of doors". As my Brother Born Divine would say, "I ain't trying to be a broke nigga in a field jacket". In this society it is imperative that an economic base is built not only to fight, but for mere survival. I hear some folks say that we could just barter like back in the days of old. In theory that sounds great. However, in practice, unless you live in a liberated zone on sovereign land with an abundance of resources that you control, then bartering alone is not going to get it. It takes dough to make bread. Keep it real; unless you are willing to knock off banks and armored trucks on a regular basis, then you need some form of financial stability. I often hear poor grassroots representatives criticizing these mega churches, the Nation of Islam, NAACP and others for their get money tactics; you could love it or leave it but, the fact is these organizations/institutions are not broke. I'm not saying that you have to subscribe or see eye to eye with any of their beliefs, but you damn sure need to figure out how you can fuel the vehicle you are attempting to drive or its going to be a long walk. Something else that must be addressed is the ridiculous notion that because a person is involved in "The Struggle" or "The Movement" then that means that they should give all of their talents or services away for free. That type of backward thinking is one of the reasons why many of the Elders are broke today. I am by no means suggesting that we become aspiring capitalists, we are very

35

aware of the lies of capitalism. Capitalism is a parasitical system designed to suck the lives out of the victims who have been duped or forced into keeping it afloat at their own expense. We know that in order for capitalism to thrive their has to be an oppressed and oppressor; someone has to be at the bottom to be stepped on by those at the top. From an Afrikan scientific socialist perspective it is our duty to build in a way that will ensure that all parties will benefit. Some folks will try to talk you into something for nothing. Donate to their cause just because. The same people that would approach you in that manner- would turn around in the same vein and tell you to "Support Black" or "Buy Black"...You can't play both sides of the fence, what's good for the goose is good for the gander. If you expect to be paid for your work, then you should treat your people the same. Pay a person their worth and if you can't then before they render their goods or services then make an agreement that can be mutually beneficial, whether its bartering or whatever other terms that is agreed upon. You can't say you are for the people and then try to get over on the people. Our success depends on our unity. It is important to not get caught up in a capitalist frame of mind, moving in a selfish, individualistic manner. Organization is key! I recommend that you find an organization to support, one that sustains the people in dire periods and if you find an organization that needs work, then work it out. It takes teamwork in order to win the game.

Sustainable Living

These days and times, I am a strong advocate of cooperatives, whether it is cooperative economics, cooperative farms, food coops or what have you. Listed below are a few basic platforms that you can begin to develop today to improve your community situation as a whole.

Susu- Susu is a cooperative economic system with West African origins in which each individual or household agrees to put up a certain dollar amount once a week or once a month. At the end of each period a different individual or household receives the money. The process repeats until all participants have benefited. For example, if there are 10 participants and each one invested $20 a week then each week a different person would receive $200.

Community or Urban Farming- All through the inner cities of this country there are Brothers and Sisters of all ages who are participating in planting, gardening and farming. Whether its growing fruits and vegetables in small cartons in their window sills, gardening in their backyards or cleaning up a plot of land in the community; agriculture is key when it comes to not only our survival, but aiding in our fight to protect the environment. If you can't find people in your community who are already practicing urban farming, get with your comrades and start making it happen. In Atlanta, our Comrades Habesha are a great example of urban farmers. During planting season they get together once a week with men, women and children of all ages to plant and tend to the crops that they work outside of a local community center. They also have courses and classes in which they educate our people on how to become urban farmers. Habesha and The FTP Movement are teaming up to not only grow food for the community, but to assist in our plight to fight hunger around the city.

Food Coops- Another way to support the community as a whole is to develop and operate a food coop or buyers club. A food coop is a beautiful way to cut out the corporate supermarkets that sell our people death. There are several types of food coops, the most popular requires a membership in which the members own and operate the coop. The members volunteer their time and energies to order materials and maintain the day-to-day operations. The members put in a certain dollar amount and buy food, toiletries and household product that are healthier and in many cases purchased from independent local producers, farmers etc. The benefits of a food coop are having a support group to living a healthier way of life and keeping your resources circulating within the community. The beauty of this type of concept is you don't have to start with a full blown food coop, you can actually start a buyers club with a few friends and just focus on things that you commonly use such as toothpaste, toilet paper and water. Just simply buying together in bulk can make a fundamental change in your financial situation.

Home schooling- Our people often complain about the lack of quality education that public schools have to offer. Many of the people that grumble have never been to a PTA meeting or let alone ventured out into independent schooling. The only time they show up at their child's school is when there is an issue or report card day. I know some folks that say they can't afford the Afrikan centered schools for their children but, their children have all the latest fashions, video games, electronic gadgets, cd's etc., (style over substance). One budding development that I'm noticing amongst concerned parents is home schooling. Home schooling is great particularly during the elementary and in some cases junior high school years. The FTP Movement has a program called Mama's Army and one of the support conduits offered is partnered home schooling. Partnered home schooling is great for those parents who can't afford to not work some type of job that would allow them the comfort of homeschooling on their own.

Community Consignment Shops- Since we know that food, clothes and shelter are basic necessities needed to live in this country and most others, you may want to look into developing a consignment shop where the people can sell or trade in their used or unused items such as clothes, furniture, books, music and other goods. It is also a decent way to raise money for your group or family unit as a whole.

RANTING AND RAVING

What the fuck ya'll looking at?

Looking at me like I'm some type of ranting, raving, lunatic

Cause I'm screamin' fuck they laws & bangin' on the gov't.

Oh now you mad?

You wanna come after me and blast me-

But when the pigs cause Black casualties

You wanna walk away casually.

Whispering, gossiping & shit-ain't that a bitch!

While Sistahs and Brothas domes is getting split,

Niggas thinking bout getting rich, in the hood we pop shit,

When pigs and white folks come around ya tone switch.

I got an itch, I got an itch I can't scratch-

I got an itchy trigga Finger and

I'm slowly caressing my gat.

And I so solemnly swear on my kinky naps-

That I'll put a hole in the laps of any frontin' ass Blacks,

That refuse to fight back, got that?

Fuck around and get ya skull cracked!

I ain't the one-I ain't the one.

Knuckle game or hammer cocked,
I'll leave you holier than Rev. Run.

Riot Starter-"Hell Yeah", like a RBG remix w/ Jigga
I'm nice with the trigga on a Harlem Night, like
Richard Pryor and that other funny nigga.

Heads a roll, souls, I deliver. Concrete guerilla thrilla,
Rebel slug dealer, any given pig killa
FTP 4 LIFE-Nuggah!

Beyond the fashionable militancy and empty rhetoric

"I'm part of a righteous people who anger slowly, but rage undamned. We'll gather at his door in such a number that the rumbling of our feet will make the earth tremble."

-George Jackson

When it comes to fighting tyranny and oppression in America, Black folks conjure up every thought in the world to avoid obligatory confrontation. Yet at the same time, like a broken record, we hear the tired old songs, "Black people need to stick together" and "We need to unite". Black people are sticking together-we are being stuck together in these penitentiary stockades and cemeteries. We unite all the time around party, bullshit and anything detrimental to our survival. I am a realist; I know that *All* Black people will never unite and that anyone telling you different is living in a fantasy world. All Black people aren't going to stick together because some Black people don't even want to be Black or Afrikan or anything else that reminds them of their scattered legacy. Some of our people prefer engaging in the sidetracking of the slave, chosing to deal with semantics and dialectology opposed to laboring to repair the damage. That's just a fact. Trying to unite all Black people is a waste of time and I don't know about you but my time is valuable. So should we just give up? Is it hopeless? Of course not. Anyone fully comprehending the austerity of our situation knows that we have to unite with others who think like us, who move like us and who have the same or similar goals as us. If you have 10 people that are down, 10 people that are dedicated and absolutely serious, then you have more than most. Its not about quantity, it's about quality. A lot of groups brag about the number of adherents they have or the number of chapters they have. What matters is how many of them are ready to do whatever it takes to be victorious. Even when the Black Panther Party was at the height of it's realm, there was only a percentage that were really keeping things in tact. Every member wasn't a straight go getter, you had some who were "Rally Panthers". These were the Panthers that came out when it was a special event or function. So when I hear someone talk about what they used to do for their people back in the 60's, I take that in consideration, but more importantly is what are you doing for your people today and what do you plan to do for them tomorrow. I respect what people say they have done, but the proof is in the "put in". I don't have time to be rappin' with no Movement drop-outs. And on the same token everybody needs somebody. No man or woman was put on this planet to live alone, we all must work together to be successful anything outside of that is a detriment to our existence. No man who has made any significant transformation in history has achieved it without a team. Isa, Mohammed, Garvey, Selassie, Martin, Malcolm all had a squad, whether you knew their names or not. No man is an Island.

We make excuses not to fight and as Imam Jamil says, "Excuses only benefit the excuse maker". Instead of some of our people acknowledging that we are oppressed and that we have the same oppressor, they wanna talk about our differences. They wanna know whether you are a Christian, Muslim, Hebrew, Moor, Buddhist or whatever. They wanna know whether you are a Nationalist, Pan Afrikanist, 5% or anything else so that we can argue about who the Original Man is as if you will escape persecution because of your belief system. They wanna ponder about where civilization began. The reality is no matter what you call yourself, how you pray, or what your personal politic is, we suffer from the same tribulations and the same subjugation. Don't aid the adversaries of our very existence by further driving a wedge between whatever commonalities we may have left. I don't care what your belief or practice is, let's deal with our common rivals first and then we could straighten out whatever other dissimilarities we may have devised. It's not about the label it's the content that matters. Khallid Abdul Muhammad used to say, "When a wino goes to buy wine, he doesn't care about the label, he wants to know can it get him drunk". So again, whatever it is you call yourself; it should be substance over style. Unfortunately, Niggas don't wanna be free; they just wanna look good, literally and figuratively. Now, I know that some people have a problem with the word "Nigga" (no matter how it's spelled). Truth is, I have a lot of folks outside the so-called "conscious community", that refer to me as "they're nigga", and treat me like a Brother, while some folks in the conscious community call me Brother, yet they treat me like a nigga. So, if we want to talk about not using certain words, then why don't we just drop English as a whole seeing that nearly the entire language is etymologically wretched.

Some folks think that the Movement is some sort of avant-garde costume gala. Dress to kill and Au Naturale. Adorned in Afrikan cultural garb, which usually consists of kente cloth, a head wrap, Che Guevara, Huey P., Assata Shakur or Angela Davis T-shirt with a stern mug to match! The more daring wannabe revolutionary thug steps on the scene equipped with an RBG wrist band, "suited and booted" with some ashy fatigues misquoting a legitimate freedom fighter, while trying to assure the people that he's ready to bust the guns he does not possess- when in reality he knows fuckin' well he won't bust a concord grape in a fruit fight. What's worse is you got folks that will recycle someone else's name, have no relationship or affiliation, destroy their legacy and no one says anything. No respect, no protocol and no accountability. Attending a meeting, rally or panel discussion sometimes reminds you of a stage show. It's like going to The Movement's equivalent of a down home church service or gospel concert. Close your eyes and you could hardly tell the difference between today's activist and a tv evangelist. It's all about the hype, the design and the dramatics. There are tons of folks who love to hear themselves speak (even if no one else wants to hear them). Instead of offering solutions to the problems that plague our community, today's activist merely finds new improved ways to "rob the dead". Capitalizing and advancing off of the suffering of the people. Mr. Black Nationalist/Pan Afrikan/Revolutionary comes in with the most rugged punch lines and a well rehearsed, stellar performance, gives a great feel good speech and offers nothing concrete. Nothing tangible and nothing practical. My people, the lost souls in search of a Black Messiah, for that moment in time gets hype and when they leave they return to reality. They return to the bitter reality of poverty, hopelessness and despair. It's like a drug, a quick fix. A high designed to temporarily take us away from the pain, but as usual after the feelings are gone, as the song goes, "where do we go from here". We are in a sad state of existence. Our people are still on a fantasy voyage to find that one hint of hope from a liar, a pimp, a thief, a snake or a con. Your Black leadership.

With the internet playing such a major role in everyday life, from dissemination of propaganda to research many so-called activists, arm chair revolutionaries, moopies (movement groupies), facebook freedom fighters, and youtube scholars have made a name for themselves by selling wolf tickets and disrespecting others like the movement for self determination is a rap battle. In these days and times your level of activism is judged by how many thumbs up you get on facebook or how many youtube hits a person receives, not on how much actual work you do. Airwaves are all the way polluted. If it's not some bullshit pumpin' through the lame stream airwaves via ClearChannel or Viacom, it's a mis-educated, wannabe intellect on blogtalk. Don't get me wrong, I'm all for freedom of speech, but at least know what you are talking about. The internet can actually serve as the "get indicted hotline". You actually have folks that share every detail of their lives through so-called social networks between facebook, myspace, and twitter you can pretty much do a psychological evaluation of a person. You have some folks that totally broadcast everything from their religion, philosophies, on the minute locations, relationships and even when they use the bathroom. Facebook makes it easier for the FBI, CIA and other so-called authorities to build their files against you. In fact Facebook is a do-it-yourself dossier against you. The feds have less work to do because so many of these "twitt-iots" as Professor Griff would say, document every move they make good or bad. On Facebook, you can even include your pictures to further aid in the state's case against you. The sad thing about it is that you have folks perpetrating the fraud, posing as bonafide revolutionaries and activists while putting out heavy duty misinformation. Unfortunately a lot of their followers don't know the difference between real and Memorex. So much pyrite laced activists "droppin' jewels" trying to shine, meanwhile the true freedom fighters are for the most part unknown. I guess in the grand scheme of things, that's not a bad thing…The sheer arrogance and utter ignorance that some of these people communicate is unbelievable. I see some of these folks who I have known for years who have declared themselves "revolutionaries" and freedom fighters gas the people up so much that even they began to believe their own hype. I know dudes that 4 or 5 years ago they were good poets at best, now they are making attempts to write themselves off as "leading scholars of our time", as if all of us have short attention spans. It baffles me that a motherfucker that copies and paste or just outright plagiarizes other people's shit can conjure up the balls to even fathom the thought of being considered an author, let alone a leading aficianado or cultural pundit. The questiom I have to ask is, where they do that at? I read a post where a good sister I know temporarily lost her mind. The sister said she took Assata off of her wall because she felt that she is doing the same work. I met this sister about 3 years ago and she was selling her ass, now with the popularity of Youtube and Facebook, along with camera phones and other gadgets, she is now an instant revolutionary. Due to the fact that there has been no accountability, people have been able to treat the liberation movement like a whore-sleep with her when they want and leave her alone until the cameras start rolling again. Giving lectures, talking shit and doing a slide show presentation does not make you a revolutionary; it just makes you a shit talking motherfucka that does slide show presentations. If you are not training, putting together programs and working towards building institutions, then you're just talking because you have a mouth. If you are in the streets just making noise talking about "what we need to do", I'm sorry that doesn't make you a revolutionary either. I hear some of these paper tigers talking about they be in the streets. What does that mean? The homeless are in the streets, prostitutes are in the streets, pimps are in the streets. What the fuck are you doing in the streets? Some of you in defense of your malarkey may sum this up as saying, "he's just a hater", and your observation would be correct. I am a hater of the bullshit you are feeding the people. Instead of updating your Facebook page and Twitter information every 5 minutes that valuable time (that you can never get back) should be spent reading a book or learning some political education from some Original Guerrillas that have experienced what you are pretending or thinking you may wanna go through. It reminds me of a quote from the "West India Emancipation" speech Frederick Douglas delivered on August 3, 1857, when he said, *"If there is no struggle there is no progress. Those who profess to favor freedom and yet deprecate agitation are men who want crops without plowing up the ground; they want rain without thunder and lightning. They want the ocean without the awful roar of its many waters"*. The audacity of folks to really play with the liberation struggle, capitalizing off of the suffering of the people in the name of a dollar or some props, exploitation of the people's legacy is ancestral treason at its finest. Let me be clear with you, since the name of this book is *How to Build a People's Army*, I don't want to play around with us. I understand that everyone that comes into our cipher is not necessarily gonna be fully committed to our struggle. We will always have "the rally panthers" that are going to be around for the special events, the cool programs, and photo opportunities. At first, I would get upset because of the fact that they were using our efforts as an attempt to make a name for themselves, but after meditating on it, I took a page from corporate America. When they don't have the manpower to keep their production up and to meet their quotas they bring in temp workers and so it is with the liberation movement, when we don't have enough builders and you have the "for the movement" folks and sympathizers you have to work them. When I say put them to work, I'm not talking about putting them in a position where they can cause damage. We must train them for specific tasks, just as a temp worker would get quick lessons on particular tasks that must be completed. If you keep working them long enough, keep them busy long enough, they will either get on the right path or fall off. It's like what Imam Jamil Al-Amin said about agents posing as Muslims to try and infiltrate the Mosque, "They keep bumpin' their heads against the floor 5 times a day (in prayer), either they're gonna become Muslim or it's gonna drive them crazy". There was a point when I had gotten fed up with people coming out to be in photos and videos when we were organizing community efforts, demos and such, so I had asked that no cameras be allowed. After discussing the matter with O.G's, they suggested that I keep it moving and document as many public pieces as possible for historic purposes.

Too often the people confuse cosmetics and costumes with the liberation struggle. What you wear is not going to get you freedom. Indeed natural hair, Afrikan garb and images that reflect us is good for the spirit of things, however it takes more than a natural and a dashiki to win us over. Revolution is NOT sexy! As El Hajj Malik El Shabazz stated, "A revolution is bloody, it knows no compromise". If bullets flying over your head, being imprisoned, being beaten, tortured, choking on your own blood and having your children snatched away from you is sexy-then I stand corrected. Now a person may say, a revolutionary is sexy, I will give you that, but anyone truly living the life of a freedom fighter knows that there may be days when they may not have the luxury of a hot shower, a meal or even housing. Until you have been on the run, living in an unfamiliar area where you can't come out until nightfall to get your meal out of a garbage can in order to survive, don't tell me about any sexy revolution! Ask Dr. Che Guevara, Reverend Nat Turner, or Field Marshal Dedan Kimathi, the beauty is in the victory not in your costume. The only time Che Guevara wore a mask was strictly for survival purposes not to be cute. Why am I so hard on the people? I know some of them don't know any better right? At least they are trying right? Wrong. I am hard on our people just as I am hard on myself. When we let bullshit go unchecked we open up holes for counterinsurgency to seep into. While some are frolicking and just want to "sell the movement", we are still being murdered and hit with football numbers. So we must address the bullshit, because we know that liberalism will

49

kill a movement quicker than a bullet will. Aside from that, we must address and make efforts to correct contradictions before they spread and the masses internalize them. On numerous occasions we have had to step to organizers and organizations about actions or inactions that have or have had the potential to damage the hearts and minds of the people. There have been occasions that the followers of the organizers and the organizations didn't agree or rather didn't understand the actions taken, however in many cases the adherents would later come to us saying that they understood and agreed with the moves that were made.

A few important jewels necessary in Building a People's Army:

Protocol-In any respectable group, organization or situation there is an established code or procedure. This is the *protocol*. Protocol is compulsory because without it there can be no real structure. For example within the ranks of a People's Army a specific proxy may serve as the spokesperson for the unit. So that basically means that just because you "feel like speaking" or you "know what to say" or even if you "felt like doing something" or you "know what to do"-if you are not sanctioned and operate outside of the approved process, then it would be considered a breach of protocol. How do you prevent violating protocol if you don't know something is protocol? Ask someone in a position of authority.

Discipline-the truism "practice makes perfect" is one that is often echoed however, in everyday life it is rarely heeded. To have discipline requires the practice of self-control, responsibility and accountability thru mental and physical training. When you are disciplined you have the ability to stay on your path or course without being swayed by ego, peer pressure or any other outside forces. Knowing that you have certain responsibilities beyond the individual, you are clear that you are to be held accountable for any inadequacies or miscarriages on your behalf.

Political Education- Political education defines our message, ideology and stance. Political education classes are necessary for the mental, spiritual and physical development of an organization, cadre, unit, or individual to ensure that comrades are on the same accord. It is necessary for organizers to have an understanding as to who and what they are fighting for. It is virtually impossible to "Know the enemy" without it. A lack of

51

political education can be disastrous and the results are a guaranteed loss. When we speak of political education, we are not just speaking of electoral politics. We are talking about the politics of liberation as a whole. It defines and educates us on our ancestors, past organizations and our current freedom fighters (i.e. movements & organizations).

Structure Fortification- Organized formations should meet at least once a week to go over the particulars of the group whether its program developments, progress or whatever issues that need to be addressed. All meetings should start promptly at a designated time. Minutes should be taken and a prearranged agenda to follow should be made available.

Regularly scheduled meetings ensure that members embrace and internalize the structure as a way of life. Punctually arriving at the meetings, establishes a uniform starting time. Taking minutes documents and reminds the assemblage of their responsibilities for its daily and monthly programs and procedures, which in turn defines its own growth from a historical perspective. A well-defined agenda aids in setting viable goals that will motivate the squad to continue to advance. Proper planning and preparation guarantees a sharper execution. ATM!

Its called Survival...

Whenever you want to get the attention of the poor and oppressed masses in America you have to speak their language. The one language in which the majority of the masses understand is food, clothes and shelter. The capitalism induced havoc that has been wreaked upon the average citizen in this country has left many "poor, raggedy and out of doors". In the 20th century we had a number of great exemplars that have provided a blueprint to combat socio-economic issues that interrupt the flow of our communities. The Honorable Marcus Mosiah Garvey and the UNIA unquestionably provided the ultimate prototype for many movements and freedom fighters to come. One of Garvey's most effective programs was the Anti-Poverty Program, which provided Blacks with sustenance that enabled many to survive during the "Great Depression" and beyond. A few years later, Elijah Muhammad and the Nation of Islam adopting similar tactics championed a "Do for self" war cry that awakened and invigorated many Black men and women, encouraging them to farm and to create their own businesses amongst other things. Continuing the development of Survival Programs, The Black Panther Party under the leadership of Huey P. Newton, Bobby Seale and others established free medical clinics, clothing drives, communal housing and a free Breakfast Program that the US government (the same government that declared war on them) mimicked and implemented in their schools. When explaining the Survival Programs, Huey P. Newton stated, "The Survival Programs are not the end all means, but it is like a raft to get the people to dry land where they can do better."

Nearly four decades later, with hunger and homelessness at an all-time high and America's failure to provide basic necessities for it's own citizens, The FTP Movement sprung into action. Inspired by the UNIA's

Anti-Poverty Program and the Black Panther Party's free breakfast program, the FTP Movement birthed the Feed The People Program.

The Feed The People program was developed out of a sense of urgency to provide nourishment for those less fortunate who have fallen through the cracks of society. Those families who have been rendered homeless courtesy of the states abandonment and the federal governments blatant disregard for human life. Launched in Atlanta, GA, in June of 2004, the Feed The People Program has spread and served over 100,000 meals and care packages in places such as Los Angeles, San Diego and parts of Canada to name a few. Care packages that include –toothpaste, soap, shampoo, deodorant, diapers and various feminine hygiene products. The mission of the Feed the People program is not to provide a crutch or to create a welfare state of mind, but to aid in the resurrection of a downtrodden people and at the same time heighten the contradictions of the "richest and greatest nation in the world". For instance, the fact that one person can possess a billion dollars and at the same time there are one billion people starving on the planet is insane. A situation such as this should be considered criminal and in a civilized society, someone should be arrested, charged with betrayal and placed on trial in front of the people.

History of the FTP Movement's Feed The People Program

On Wednesday June 9, 2004, "The Dusk Daughters" (Comrades Meshaniyah and Oluremi) and I went out to a weekly poetry/open mic event at The Black Lion Café on historic Auburn Avenue (down the street from Martin Luther King's house, church and place of burial) to promote what would be our first event in Atlanta; Poets 4 Political Prisoners. At the time, this particular open mic was being held every Wednesday night between 9 pm - 11pm. While out, we bumped into Malikah Hameen a poet who had contacted us about a week before inquiring about performing at our Poets 4 Political Prisoners event which was to take place on June 21st. When she arrived we talked and she informed us that she had some lunches in her van that her husband had left over from his job at a day camp at a community center. She offered the poets and attendees the lunches but everyone there was too cool to accept the meals. After a while we decided that all of the homeless folks in the surrounding areas that we passed in order to get to the spot could benefit from the food. That night at about 10:45 pm, the four of us went out (along with another male poet) and passed out 120 meals to displaced Brothers and Sisters in the downtown area. What we did not know at the time was that we were in the process of initiating our first program in the Atlanta area. Seeing the number of homeless folks on the street that night and the appreciation they had for the little sustenance that we offered, inspired us to make this part of our Wednesday night regimen. Afterwards, we spoke and Malikah agreed to talk to her husband about bringing home any leftovers on Wednesdays and we would meet up at The Black Lion to distribute them. The following week we met up as agreed, announced on the microphone that after the set we would be going out to distribute food to the homeless and offered those who were in attendance the opportunity to join us in our endeavors. Some united with what we were doing, others ignored us and made it clear that they were just there to spit their "revolutionary" poems and not actually do any work that would benefit the people. For the next few weeks, we continued to push the leftover lunches until we were told that "the hookup" had run dry. Rather than end what we had just begun, we decided to solicit donations from other supporters and whatever we couldn't get from them we would put our own resources together to make it happen.

For the next several months, until October 2004 we would utilize Comrade Malikah's home as a base to prepare brown bag lunches, which would consist of sandwiches, fruit, water and other snacks and meet up with other supporters in the parking lot of the Black Lion and go around the area feeding the people. At the end of October, I spoke to the owner of The Royal Peacock a club located about a block up on Auburn Ave about utilizing his establishment as a base to meet with other allies, prepare food and disburse. The owner agreed to allow us the usage of Paradise, the restaurant located downstairs from The Royal Peacock, on Tuesday nights. The Royal Peacock was once a famous club that hosted legends like Ray Charles, James Brown and many others. It was at this new location that we expanded our operation by adding clothes and toiletries amongst other items. It was here that we began to write inspiration and educational messages on the bags and also include propaganda inside to bring about awareness. This is when our program spread like wildfire. Other organizations, sororities, fraternities, rappers, attorneys, professors, churches etc., would all come out to support our movement. We had students come from as far as Columbia University (NY) to interview us and participate to students from Clark Atlanta, Morehouse, Spelman College and Georgia State Universities coming thru to get their community service hours. In fact, Groove Phi Groove, a fraternity at Morehouse College actually adopted our program in order to get more of their students involved.

Feed The People Takes Flight

In August of 2005, Comrade Shaka At-thinnin, Chairman of The Original Black August Organizing Committee invited me to come out to Oakland, California to help promote festivities and to host the 26th Annual Black August Commemoration Concert. During that time I met a group of about a dozen or so revolutionary poets and singers called the "Nappy Tongue Vanguard". The Nappy Tongue Vanguard had traveled from Los Angeles to perform and take part in the Black August festivities as well. We kicked it off well, discussing what we were doing in our areas and I mentioned the Feed The People program and they hipped me to the homeless situation in LA. I spoke with Sadiki Bakari who was the leader of the group and he expressed interest in uniting with the FTP Movement and bringing the program to the west coast. When I returned to Atlanta, I received a telephone call from Comrade Sadiki saying that he and the NTV had discussed implementing the Feed The People program and they wanted to go over the process. That October, the group flew our Defense Captain, Commander Shakur Sunni-Ali and myself out to Los Angeles to work towards the development of a new division. Commander Shakur held an RBG training class dealing with self-defense and I spoke at a college, and a couple other venues and together we all laid out the foundation to what would become the second official chapter of The FTP Movement. One very important thing I would be remiss to mention is that whenever you touch down (or better yet before you arrive) in a city other than your own, you should always reach out to the O.G.'s

57

and other organizations that are positioned in the area. By doing so, it shows respect to those who were there before you and it also minimizes any misunderstandings as to the role you are attempting to play in that area. So before we arrived I reached out to other comrades in the vicinity and also asked that our new comrades extend the olive branch to family they knew of within range. At the first LA Feed The People we organized, there were over 50 participants, not only from the NTV but also members of one of the Moorish groups, The Black Riders and Guerilla Republik. We even had comrades from the Native Youth Movement drive down from Arizona because they knew we would be in town so they wanted to train with us and assist in the organizing process. We were quickly educated on the street politics and the electoral politics of LA. We started our mission into some of the communities trooping, chanting and supplying brown bag lunches to the people. Since we were representing the RBG with plenty of red, black & green bandanas and apparel (LA is big on identifying colors), General T.A.C.O., leader of The Black Riders made phone calls to different Blood & Crip O.G.'s giving them a heads up that we would be coming thru, so that there wouldn't be any confusion apropos the colors and our position vis-à-vis the community. This was done not out of fear but as stated above, as a sign of respect to those whose territories we were making an effort to enter into. We started off in the hood then we proceeded to Skid Row. Skid Row is an area strategically located in downtown LA filled with blocks and blocks of homeless, mentally ill and chemical substance dependent folks. The only way to describe Skid Row would be a scene from the Night of the living dead. There had to be thousands of humans confined to this one area. You could literally smell death in the air. Men, women and children sleeping on the sidewalks, dealers peddling syringes, crack stems and screens and so many homeless that the City of Los Angeles put port-apotties on every block so that the destitute citizens would have a place to relieve themselves. I witnessed women squatting on toilets on a busy city street in broad daylight using the bathroom with the door wide open like they were home alone. All the images of Beverly Hills, Hollywood and all the glitz and glamor of California made it evident that the American dream is still a nightmare to the have not's, the hungry and the colonized.

After instituting foundations in both Atlanta and Los Angeles we began to establish a presence online and throughout a myriad of communities via various social networks and thru "friendly media" along with the aid of supporters sympathetic to our cause, The FTP Movement began to spread like wildfire with members and chapters sprouting up globally.

How to organize a Feed The People Program in your area:

Organizing a Feed The People program is a rather simple process. The first thing that you would want to do is make an assessment and pinpoint parts of your city that are inundated with displaced individuals. If you are uncertain as to where the most people gather, you may want to ask around or drive around early in the morning and towards the evening and take notes as to whether there are a majority of men, women or entire families. You may also want to get a list of the various shelters located around town. Next you should reach out to your organization, friends, associates and co-workers about getting involved in the plight to end homelessness and hunger. Then you want to make a list of some of the things that you know the people can use. For example, if its winter time you know hot meals, blankets, and coats would be useful, if you are uncertain as to what would be needed put yourself in their shoes and think of basic essentials that you would need in a situation such as this. From there, you and your people can make a list of any low-priced or wholesale marketplaces that you could purchase supplies or that may donate to your cause. Each individual can chip in $5-$10 to procure the goods or contribute from their own stash. Another way is to either have food/clothing drives on your jobs or at your schools. As far as clothing, you can ask participants; neighbors and associates to donate can goods, gently worn clothing, blankets and other articles that would be useful. Next, you want to secure a meet-up location to prepare the food, and to sort the clothing and hygiene kits. One very important footnote is that the purpose of the Feed The People program should not be to create a welfare type dependency where handouts are expected or to cultivate another charity program but to aid, educate, politicize and heighten the contradictions of the so-called leaders of the "free world".

A list of supplies that you may need:

Bread (preferably wheat or unbleached)
Peanut butter
Jelly
Cold Cuts- turkey/chicken bologna (no pork or beef)
Tofurkey (non-meat cold cuts)
Condiments (mayonnaise/mustard)
Fruit (bananas/apples/oranges/peaches/plums etc.)
Snacks (potato chips, boxes of raisins etc.)
Water (individual bottles)
Juice (individual bottles)
Sandwich Bags
Brown Paper Bags (Lunch size)
Plastic Grocery Bags (to carry lunches for distribution)
Plastic utensils (for condiments)

For Hot Meals (non-perishables):

Can Goods
Rice
Dry Beans
Soup
Hot Chocolate
Tea
Spaghetti (and pasta sauce)
Containers (Styrofoam or plastic)
Paper Plates
Aluminum Foil or Plastic Wrap
Plastic utensils
Cups
Napkins
Sternos (liquid heat to keep the food warm)

Toiletries:
Toothpaste
Toothbrushes

Soap
Deodorant
Shampoo
Lotion
Disposable Razors (men and women)
Shaving Cream
Nail Clippers
Socks
Underwear
Diapers (and baby formula)
Feminine Hygiene Products

Clothing Articles:
Pants/Shirts
Shoes
Sweaters
Coats
Thermal Underwear
Gloves
Hats
Scarves
Blankets

On the lunch bags you may want to write positive or political messages such as "feed the people", "free the prisoners" "for the people" etc. Inside of the bags you may want to include a mission statement or other forms of propaganda to educate and inspire the recipients.

*One final note is that when you are caravanning thru the city and are stopping at different locations you want to provide participants with a map of the areas you will be covering and also ask that all drivers keep their hazard lights on when mobile so that drivers that may fall behind would know that you are together (especially when participants are not familiar with all of the vehicles).

CONCRETE BLUES

Confusion within inspired by a whirlwind of life's pressure
A combination of pain & pleasure, beyond measure-
This world will test ya- I keep an Ankh and a 9mm on my
dresser
For those who choose to stress the

Black Power, No compromising –bullshit despising
Poor freedom fighting wise man
Whose goal is to continue rising

And inspire poor righteous souls with
their back up against the wire
And their hearts on fire.

I've cried so much that the water is overflowing
And now you could see the rain outside my window-

I feel like Mr. Wendall in Tennessee-
Trying to set my mind free.

Concrete Blues the Mutha fuckin' Hood News,
Baby need new shoes, and out of the hand off Renae
My dope fiend neighbor, blood and pus ooze-

While the pigs cruise & young boys
Clutch their jewels and tuck their tools
Screamin' "fuck the rules", pass the
Menthol Kools or box of Newports.

They hit my Brother with arrearage.
He's late again with child support-
Back to court.

My auntie just wanted one more snort,

Now her lifeline abort.

And allow me to retort about these mutha fuckas
Arguing about a gay marriage- the other day
I saw 2 white men holding hands and smoking cigarettes,
while one pushed two black girls in a carriage-

Although they looked happier than average,
I'm sorry but them mutha fuckas still living life savage.
I saw a negro beggin' for change with a mouthful of 18
karats,
I had to grin and bear it,
He tried to sell me a picture of the pope,
I tried to grab that shit & tear it...

I said, if the truth fits wear it,
He wasn't trying to hear it.

I'm a rebel to Amerikkka and mf's fear it,
If I was a fly ass suit a living dead man
Wouldn't wanna wear it.

Flesh of my flesh- I got soul in my spirit.
My pen & paper have a holy matrimony and
Marriage without prenuptials-

The words I recite make people uncomfortable.
If you just listen to my shit the feds will wanna hunt you.

Concrete Blues, petty bourgeoisie Negroes want to exploit
My talents, but they can't cause that bullshit is invalid.

Some mutha fuckas round the way, want beef with me, But
I prefer a salad.
You'll be a damn fool trying to step to me with a challenge.

Freedom fighting that's all I know.
I carefully pick my words so they could spread out like an
Afro,
It's only natural.

I got the People's back like Che Guevara and
Fidel Castro or H. Rap & Stokely.
Don't provoke me.

My words so strong if I don't get
Them out the verbs and nouns might choke me.

By any means necessary, we will use whatever
Methods or tools. We refuse to loose,

Even if we have to give Bush cement shoes, Nothings
Gonna stop us from escaping these goddam,
Concrete Blues!

Class Struggle

"A revolution is not a dinner party, or writing an essay, or painting a picture, or doing embroidery; it cannot be so refined, so leisurely and gentle, so temperate, kind, courteous, restrained and magnanimous. A revolution is an insurrection, an act of violence by which one class overthrows another"-Mao Tse Tung

An invaluable lesson that every organizer has to learn and understand is ideaology around class struggle. Not just the class struggle between the ruling class and the masses, but class struggle amongst the organizations and organizers. Oftentimes we take for granted that because we are all fighting the same fight that we are all looking to use the same methods or expect the same results. Kwame Ture used to say, "Everybody fighting for the same thing may not necessarily be against the same thing and everybody against the same thing may not necessarily be for the same thing". Class struggle often stems from a need for some to hold on to their acquired petit bourgeious tendencies which have been deeply rooted thru socioeconomic status, education and thinking while another cluster may denounce such societal strata altogether. When it all boils down, whats left may be the difference in having something to lose and having nothing to lose. In class struggle you may have some that can only go so far because there may be a fear of losing their security. Security in the form of careers, relationships, prestige, material objects, or insignificant trinkets handed down by the very same autocrat that they profess to be against. The four centuries of captivity coupled with Jim Crow has done such an outstanding job on the warping and dismantling of the minds of the people that even those who are displeased and rebellious still subconciously hold on to the burning string of capitalism. Its like the song goes, "Everybody wanna go to heaven, but they don't wanna die". Countless petit bourgeois elements speak of being in "the trenches" but in reality they have no interest in touching the soil. Many would rather skinny dip in proverbial waters of a flimsy façade of respectability, rather than engage in fisticuffs to procure their rightful position in civilization. They step into the arena talking like Don King, "Its us against them" but, when the heat gets turned up they began to sound like Rodney King, "Can't we all just get along?". If granted the opportunity, you can rest assure that there are some that would spend the rest of their days rubbing elbows with the elite, high society and upperclass and will forget the interest of the poor and working class that they think they are thinking about representing. Some may view it as hypocrisy however, I look at it as learned behavior in which the oppressor has been the best teacher. We have to have patience and understand that our people are looking at the world thru European eyes, thinking and dreaming with European minds, and all the while fighting for self determination to maintain what little Afrikan identity we have manged to salvage. Indeed a complex undertaking that only a few are willing to endure. In the words of Mao, "We should support whatever the enemy opposes and oppose whatever the enemy supports".

Class struggle is so thick you can cut it with a knife. Class struggle is so heavy that if you don't move a certain way, dress a certain way, or talk a certain way, one risks the chance of being ostracized by their so-called contemporaries. An example would be the City of Atlanta. When I first moved to Atlanta in 2004, I noticed class struggle right off the rip. Of course there's always class struggle amongst the masses, like our Brother Stic from the group dead prez said in his song, "Everybody wanna be somebody, better than everybody". However, when I moved to Atlanta, the invisible line between the Cultural Nationalist, The Black Nationalist and the Pan Afrikanist was as clear as the text on this page. I quickly understood that the city in which some refer to as "The Black experience" is really a Black experiment. It's the place where they imprisoned Marcus Garvey, H. Rap Brown, Dr. Mutulu Shakur, Kamau Sadiki and so many others. It's where 29 Black children mostly male, were experimented on and murdered. It's where they assassinated Khallid Abdul Muhammad. It's where the CDC operates a $214 million dollar experimental infectious disease facility (adjacent to The Emory University Campus). And it's also the capital of black homosexuality, with Morehouse and Spelman Colleges, all male and all female Campuses serving as an incubator. From the bottom to the top, it's a well dressed system of subjugation. So much so that the transplanted Afrikan comes in and actually forgets he or she is in the very racist State of Georgia, that is until he or she either runs into the police and they beat them silly or until they venture to the outskirts, and is quickly reminded by the down home racist that, "You Ain't in Atlanta boy-you in Georgia". I like to compare Atlanta to a well furnished lion's mouth. A lion's mouth with plush carpet, a nice living room set, and expensive furniture, well decorated for your comfort. You forget you are in a lion's mouth, until of course the lion begins to devour you and then it's too late. The so called "liberation movement" in Atlanta is quite similar. It has little if anything to do with what you know or who you know-it's about who likes you and who doesn't. A strange place where cultural nationalism and intellectual masturbation reign supreme. No consideration for any type of protocol. You can literally do what you like without any consequences, just dress the part and don't ruffle any feathers. You have a few self appointed, clown-shoe wearing organizations that consider themselves "The Vanguard of the Struggle". Distinguished, elite, very special, intellectual, vegetarian lollipop, flip flop, dreadlock neo-Negroes who speak as if they have "arrived". Talking just because they have mouths with philosophies so "deep" that they don't walk they levitate. And in many cases the "elders" are qualified as Elders due to age not because of knowledge, wisdom or active participation in community building. Don't misunderstand me; I am by no means throwing slugs at the place where I rest, nor am I attempting to disrespect those who are worthy of respect. Lames exist all over the planet; I am simply using this City as an example, because this is where I am based. It is a very frustrating situation when you have so many beautiful yet confused Black people. There are certainly some real live Soldiers and Generals in Atlanta; unfortunately the level of counterinsurgency keeps them off the scene. But regardless their presence is still felt and that's why we continue to fight here, in the mouth of the lion. Peace to All Those Who Do Good.

Encountering other organizations or troops:

When dealing with other organizations if you are in a position of leadership and there is a contradiction with a member or members of another organization, the matter should be taken to the leadership of that organization immediately. If you are a member of an organization and you have a situation with a member of another organization, then the first thing you should do is approach your leadership, making them aware of the situation at hand at which time you should receive instructions from the proper chain of command. If your leadership is not present and they cannot be reached, and conflict is avoidable then you should stand-down until you receive instructions from leadership. If conflict is unavoidable and there are more than one of you on site then the person with the most experience should assume leadership. Going about it in this manner is one way to limit the possibility of a problem escalating. Our goal should be to avoid conflict with comrades and allies. We must keep in mind that our issue is with the oppressor not the oppressed. We understand the enemies of the people will always send in agent provocateurs to disrupt, discredit and destroy any movement that threatens their system of domination and destruction. With set protocols and procedures, bullshit can be weeded out before it is allowed to fester and grow. We have to be able to operate whether our adversaries are present or not.

Organizational Courtesy:

The leadership of an organization serves as a representative of their faction just as a leader of a nation represents their realm. It is proper civility to treat the leadership of an organization with a degree of respect that should be awarded to any dignitary. Elders, O.G's, and organizational leaders should always be acknowledged and treated honorably regardless of whether you agree personally or whether or not you agree with their particular political line. The way one interacts with an individual in a leadership position is a clear indication of the level of respect or lack of respect that individual may have. Certainly, respect is a two-way street. The leader is granted the degree of respect not because he is better or above the people, but because of his service and rank. An example of a basic level of respect is not having Elders, O.G's, and organizational leaders wait in line at special events or other gatherings, for security purposes. It is also the duty of the particular leader's group to make sure that a representative is sent to alert the security at the door that the leadership has arrived and as a safety precaution should be granted immediate access. The leadership must be respected. If there is no respect for the leadership, there will be no respect for the organization.

CRITICISM AND SELF-CRITICISM: THE METHOD OF ORGANIZATIONAL SELF-DEVELOPMENT

Lessons from Mao Tse Tung

In the development of a revolutionary organization, it is necessary to discuss the method used for internal growth and development. Being a political organization that represents the interest of Afrikan people, we must attempt to be responsible for our actions and to the people at all times. To keep ourselves from becoming an isolated cultural nationalist or revolutionary cult, we must engage ourselves in criticism and self-criticism. Through criticism and self-criticism defects can be discovered and corrected, while good qualities can be further developed.

We must be willing to admit and correct faults, and fight against political stagnation. Criticism and self-criticism should be considered a part of our revolutionary practice. It is part of our nation-building process, which makes us into more politically developed, humble servants of the people.

Criticism and self-criticism is one of our daily necessities. A revolutionary organization or cadre can't live without criticism and self-criticism. It consolidates revolutionary organization, activates the revolutionary organization, activates the individual revolutionary, and gives added strength. The development of the revolution demands our raising and training cadre. Apart from establishing schools, this training must be done by criticism and self-criticism to achieve a general improvement in political ideology.

Deviations in Criticism and Self-Criticism

- There is a type of cadre who tries to hide his faults and refuses to be honest. Although it is obvious his faults are paramount, he thinks he only has a few, and denies having any faults at all. His relationship to the organization, cadre and the people is built on false pride (ego).

No one is faultless. If you have the courage to admit your errors and correct them, the masses will respect you, not despise you.

- Some cadres are aggressive when it comes to criticizing others. They collect all sorts of hearsay and engage in a blitzkrieg. Other cadre are very casual about their own faults, glossing over the serious matters and only mentioning the petty errors, minimizing the major defects and ignoring the minor ones. This is their attitude toward themselves, but with others, their policy is one of faultfinding and exaggeration. They are lenient with themselves, but give no breathing space to others.

- Some cadres put all the emphasis on a detail and think it can express the whole. They catch on to some petty fault of this or that cadre and try to wipe him/her out with it. They collect a whole list of petty matters and totally disregard the real nature of the so-called fault, whether it was deliberate or accidental, habitual or otherwise, political or ideological, and they do not inquire about the current conditions.

- Some cadre, in criticizing others, like to bring up only the good points and avoid speaking about the faults altogether. Some of our cadres like only to hear others say how good they are; but when anyone mentions their defects, they get angry. The type of cadre, who is full of praise, is exactly to their taste. They do not understand that this type of praise is nothing but empty words.

- One deviation is only criticizing the defects and not mentioning the good points. Some think that criticism means just pointing out faults. They think that the aim of criticism is to find as many faults as possible.

- Some cadres only examine and criticize themselves, but do not criticize others. This type of cadre is solicitous about himself/herself, but careless about others.

- Then there are those who are always trying to gloss over difficulties. These people believe in making trifles out of the big things and try to dismiss smaller matters altogether.

- Some cadres like perfect peace. Their attitude toward themselves is easygoing; their attitude toward others is equally so.

- Some people, rather than criticizing a cadre to his/her face, do it all behind his/her back. Rather than doing their criticizing at meetings, they indulge in gossiping criticism after the meeting. They gossip to everyone they meet, and the only one they do not say anything to is the one they are criticizing. A good person is not afraid to speak face-o-face; but these brothers or sisters are too shy.

- Some cadre make their own personal likes and dislikes their guiding principle. With their friends, it is all mutual protection and screening. Although it is as clear as daylight that their friend has many faults, because of personal consideration, they will not criticize and even try to whitewash their friend. But with brothers and sisters they do not like, they put on a grim expression and make a special speech, and try to show that nothing that he/she can do or say is right.

- Some cadres obstinately refuse to admit their faults. When they are criticized, they deny everything.

- Some cadres, although in their hearts they accept criticism and admit their defects, fail to publicly and openly admit that they are at fault. If these cadres do not have the courage and determination to admit their faults, where will they find the resolution to correct them?

If we analyze these shortcomings, we find three incorrect ideologies: **Subjectivism, Liberalism and Cliquism.** These attitudes to criticism and self-criticism are not revolutionary attitudes. They are devoid of principle. Subjectivism is a non-materialist ideology. Liberalism is a relic of capitalist ideology and cliquism of bourgeois individualist (selfish) ideology. They are all antagonistic to the revolutionary standpoint. This type of criticism and self-criticism is not plain dealing and straightforward. It is a debased variety. It puts self first and relegates the group to second place.

It means that the ideologies of the old society and its doctrines have worked their way into revolutionary brothers and sisters to the level of personal social relations. It means turning criticism and self-criticism into a means of social intercourse. Incorrect criticism confuses the struggle of our people's enemies with internal ideological struggle, and this results in regarding one's brothers and sisters as the enemy.

Another incorrect type of criticism and self-criticism contaminates revolutionary criticism with the methods of the hoodlums of society – deception and cutthroat intimidation. These defects arise out of cadre being concerned more with their own interests than with the interests of the revolutionary cause. To give expression to these vicious habits in revolutionary criticism and self-criticism is a grave error. To contaminate the revolutionary ranks with these base ideologies, especially cliquism, is absolutely impermissible.

Developing Authentic Criticism and Self-Criticism

- We should be scrupulously honest in criticism and self-criticism. The Afrikan working class looks for truth among the facts. Our Brothers and Sisters must eliminate all vain gloriousness and self-conceit. To admit faults does not mean that you are rotten to the core. Admitting faults and revealing them to the group always pays and harms no one. Not only does it involve no "loss of face," but also on the contrary, it enhances one's prestige and increases one's influence. Frankly admitting one's faults strengthens one's connections with the masses, so of course frankness is welcome by the masses. The comrade who obstinately upholds their faults, makes allowances for themselves, or tries to argue their faults out of existence, can only isolate themselves from the masses. The masses will be dissatisfied with them and they will lose all influence with them.

- We should take a serious, not irresponsible, attitude to criticism and self-criticism. We should have the whole group at heart, because a cadre who commits faults and has defects is harmful to the revolutionary cause and also harmful to the group. Cadres must develop self-criticism and pay attention to the criticism of the group. Cadre should not make any distinction between their own faults and the faults of others. If one is tolerant of the faults of other cadres, this means ruining those cadres. Similarly, to take a lenient attitude to one's faults is ideological suicide. To uphold or tolerate faults is to add fault to fault, to nourish and promote faults.

- Cadres should uphold the guiding principle without faltering, distinguish between right and wrong, and criticize according to the guiding principle and not according to personal whims. Petty everyday matters which have no connection with principles – these things do not warrant the group's criticism and do not need to be elevated to the rank of a matter of principle.

- When criticizing a cadre, one should first admit his/her good points and then criticize his/her defects or shortcomings. Only in this way will that cadre cheerfully accept our criticism, only in this way will the aim of criticism be achieved. If one concentrates only on somebody's faults, nullifies and denies his/her merits, and makes him/her out to be altogether bad – if one takes this line, in the first place it makes it difficult for that cadre to accept any criticism at all, and secondly it makes him/her feel that he/she is worthless, devoid of any good points makes him/her disheartened and pessimistic. Of course, this does not mean listing all of a cadre's merits each time before starting to criticize his/her defects. It merely means that while criticizing someone, the fact that he/she also has good points should be kept in mind. It should be understood that criticism and self-criticism is something that everyone, without exception, should take part in.

- Cadres should be unemotional and objective in their criticism; they should be good-natured, reasonable and analytical. Indiscriminate name-calling is not needed. Emotionalism and insufficient knowledge of the facts can only result in subjectivism and narrow-mindedness. People with a petty-bourgeois background are often shortsighted in their point of view. In criticizing this or that person, or this and that matter, it is essential to distinguish between what is deliberate and what is unintentional. Only by finding out the truth from the facts, by objectively analyzing and explaining each question, can we insure that our criticism will be cheerfully and unconditionally accepted. At the same time we should point out to the cadre a road to improvement; as far as possible show him a way to correct his defects because criticism and self-criticism is not only destructive but constructive as well. Its aim is to replace petty bourgeois ideologies.

- Our attitude to our cadre should be like that of a doctor towards his patient. We should criticize in a good-natured spirit, in the spirit of helping a cadre to learn from his/her mistakes. The aim of criticizing a cadre or criticizing an undesirable phenomenon is to correct that cadre's faults and to get work done well. It is a cadre's incorrect ideology that we want to destroy, not his whole ideology. Only in this way can we encourage a cadre to overcome his defects and develop his good qualities.

- Cadres need a courageous spirit in self-criticism. We should struggle for a decisive victory on the ideological front. In criticizing others, a bold spirit is needed as well.

- Cadres should take the authentic not the extremist, line in criticism and self-criticism. We should not struggle against petty bourgeois ideologies with petty bourgeois tactics. We cannot abolish faulty ideologies as long as our own point and attitude is faulty. Cadres should not criticize from the standpoint of personal prejudice. If we try to fight faults with faults in this way, it can only result in confusion in adding fault to fault, in confusing what is right with what is wrong. So we oppose not only the philosophy of compromising with faults, but also opposite extremes. Criticism and self-criticism must be based on reason; it must have content and a guiding principle.

The revolutionary can only win the confidence of the masses and provide them with leadership if they can see that the revolutionist himself/herself is the embodiment of revolutionary humanist values. They must be able to witness in the revolutionist his/her continuous personal development and transformation into a more conscious, more human, more socially responsible man or woman, without personal self-interest, prepared to tackle the most difficult tasks, if these will help improve the conditions and heighten the political consciousness of the masses, constantly educating himself/herself so that he/she can educate others. This unceasing self-humanizing process by the revolutionist is especially necessary in the United States, a county that is so inhumane that it can even drive those in rebellion against it into inhuman acts which only demoralize the masses by confirming them in their suspicion that you can't beat the system.

Man cannot will himself/herself into birth, but once born he/she can will his/her journey to growth and maturity. The stronger and more self-conscious this will, the more planned and patterned is the process of growth. Organizations do not possess a will outside the will of their members, although they obey the same laws of growth; members of any organization should periodically subject their wills to an examination of motives and aims, for growth that neglects human will.

A snitch is a glitch in the matrix/ hatred escapes lips that twist/and turn coat against the collective/ disunity breeds dis respect for ones own community/plantation politricks house niggas still fall for the okey doke lettin babylon poke and prod they brains for a little loose change/ lookin for love in all the wrong faces- we dont need them for sh*t! The call to follow the protocol falls on deaf ears to agent provocateurs that look walk and talk like I n I but they fraudulent as vegans that eat casein/no ice for ho lice nor the mice that run in collusion/ Fiya burn dem is the conclusion/so thirsty no mercy no favors for traitors have you forgotten how the system do in original black men women children? Sleeping with the enemy breeds enmity rockin wires and star spangled drawers under dashiki and rbg/yo FED stamp is dangling from yo head wrap/the clothes don't make the revolutionary, the proof is in the put in. Stop snitchin'

IMPRESS OFFICIAL MUSIC 2009
staHHr

Loose Lips Sink Ships

"I'm from the era where niggas don't snitch, you from the era where snitchin' is the shit...
-Jay Z

One of the most popular street crusades in recent times has been the "Stop Snitchin' Campaign". The campaign made popular by what some would call a controversial DVD created by Rodney "Skinny Suge" Thomas, a recognized Baltimore, MD record producer, quickly became a national hood slogan. The low-budget street DVD, which featured an appearance by Denver Nugget basketball star Carmelo Anthony, was definitely one of the most talked about DVD's of 2004 and 2005. The most beautiful thing about the DVD was that it identified former Baltimore Police officers William A. King and Antonio L. Murray as dope pushers and thieves. King and Murray were found guilty and received 454 years in the penitentiary after an FBI investigation in 2005. Drug dealers testified that the 2 cops were involved in the use of robbery, extortion, and excessive force against various dealers as a means of reselling the drugs for profit on the street. Now that's poetic justice.

It should be noted that in response to The Stop Snitchin' DVD, the Baltimore Police department created their own campaign, "Keep Talkin'", which used free DVDs and T-shirts in a method similar to that of the Stop Snitchin' campaign. Their campaign was launched of course as an effort to keep snitchin' alive.

The Stop Snitchin' DVD followed by a series of Stop Snitchin' t-shirts spread like wildfire. The Stop Snitchin' t-shirts were cool as some of my comrades stated, "For bringing about awareness". My only concern was that all the snitches decided to buy the t-shirts to take the heat off of themselves. So in some cases the words on the shirt became just that, words on a shirt. I just could never understand why a person would have to wear a t-shirt to remind him or anyone else he knew not to snitch, thought that was a given. I guess there are no foregone conclusions. It probably would have been more on point to put out propaganda saying, "Don't feed the animals"-because too many people keep the pigs fat by feeding them info.

The slogan itself became so popular that it opened doors for people like rapper Cam'ron to get on national television and make a fool out of himself, Hip Hop and the streets. On April 22, 2007, CNN's Anderson Cooper interviewed Cam'ron on a special segment of the popular CBS news program, 60 minutes. One of the questions that Cooper asked Cam'ron was, "If you knew there was a serial killer living next door, would you call the police?" Cam'ron the hardcore, pink fur wearing gangsta replied, "I would probably just move", claiming he would not talk to the police. Now, you would think that this super-thug wannabe would call some of his team and handle the serial killer. I guess his lyrics are for entertainment purposes only. According to the NYPD, Cam'ron aka Cameron Giles didn't always have the "Don't talk to police" policy. In reports obtained by *The Smoking Gun,* New York Police Department records indicate that he cooperated with cops after he was assaulted at a Harlem playground. According to an NYPD report, Giles--who is listed as "compl," or complainant--got into a "verbal dispute" with about 15 black males "while at a basketball game" in August 1999. After they knocked him to the ground, Giles was kicked in the head and groin. Giles was debriefed by police at Bellevue Hospital, where he was treated and released... I guess he meant he only talks to police when it's convenient for him.

Now without question, No Snitchin' is at the top of The Street Codes because we are totally against it, no matter what you call it droppin' a dime, informing, dry snitchin', tattle tellin', or whatever nice way you put it, snitching is snitching. I would have never imagined that we would someday have to put on paper that snitching wasn't cool. Of course there have always been a few turncoats in the community. A few clowns that wanted to play the game then flip the script when they got jammed. Folks like "Mr. Untouchable" Nicky Barnes and "The American Gangster" Frank Lucas. Certainly Hollywood and the music industry have played its part in glorifying snitching. You have rappers snitching on themselves on records, talking about how much weight they move, guns they carry, who they shot etc. Now some of you may say "That's just entertainment". I might of went for that until recently an aspiring rapper in Georgia received 20 years for making a song about a dude he shot and actually saying the victims name admitting he shot him on record! Rico Todriquez Wright, 25, was sentenced to 20 years in jail and 20 years of probation on 2 counts of aggravated assault for shooting Chad Blue. Blue, who was permanently disabled from a bullet that hit him in his thigh and shattered in his groin was home recuperating when a friend brought a song for him to hear. In the song called, 'Hitting Licks for a Living' there's a line that says 'Chad Blue knows how I shoot'. Huh? This is when keepin' it real goes wrong. Somebody give Rico a Stop Snitchin' t-shirt. If this dude would tell on himself you know what he would do for you.

According to the streets nobody would be snitching, but you can have a cat selling drugs for 7 years and never get caught, always happen to leave before the cops come, ain't he lucky. Then there's the other dude that can get caught with 2 keys of coke, a pound of weed and an AK and be out on bail the next day. Next thing you know he got probation or a year in jail. Oh yeah, he had a good lawyer.

Its gotten so cold in Atlanta that after 92 year old Kathryn Johnston was murdered by the Atlanta Police Department (in her own home), the cops called one of their paid informants to say that the informant had bought drugs from the elderly woman's residence earlier that day.The snitch couldn't muster up the nerve to say that he brought anything, let alone drugs from this Black Woman who reminded him of his Great-Grandmother. Instead he went on the news and flipped on the police, saying that they asked him to lie to cover up the murder. He also admitted that he was a paid informant and that he snitched for as little as $20. The truth is so strong, that even a liar has to spit it out. Promised protective custody by the FBI, the "tatted up" 23 year-old Alex White's picture was on the front page of The Atlanta Journal and Constitution. Feeling like a hero Mr. White along with Markell Hutchins, an aspiring civil rights activist/preacher held a press conference in which Alex White was praised for his actions. Conveniently forgetting he was a snitch.

Soon after, White was back in the news. This time he hit the media circuit talking about how he was filing a lawsuit against the City of Atlanta.

In his federal lawsuit, Mr. White claims that he made about $25,000 annually from his work as a paid informant and that he was seeking an unspecified amount of lost wages, damages for emotional distress and attorney fees from the city and its police department. He said that his "credibility" as a confidential informant has been damaged due to the fact that his face was on television. Now he can't get a job as a confidential informant. According to a newspaper article, he said, "he was forced into hiding and he is still afraid of retribution from police and drug dealers he turned in."

Recently, Alex White was arrested in Douglas County, Georgia for allegedly selling weed to undercover agents on two different occasions. Sherriff Phil Miller of the Douglas County Police Department stated, "An informant gave us information about him and as a result of that information we were able to make two under cover buys from him". Goes to show the saying is right, there is no honor amongst thieves.

How to organize "Operation Cop Block" in your area

Operation Cop Block is a concept that was started by our comrade, Activist/Hip Hop artist Mike Flo and adopted by The FTP Movement. Cop Block is a real easy piece that can literally save our people time, money and even their lives. Great way to avoid getting your car towed or locked up by the gangbanging exploiters masquerading as "servants of the people" whose real purpose is to serve and protect the interest of the establishment. When you see the haters have set up roadblocks you send out text messages to the people in your phone so that they could avoid the trap. Make you sure you include the street or highway location. You also get everyone you know to forward it to the people in their network and so on and so forth. The same thing applies to police harassment. When you see the police abusing or violating the people's rights you forward the text messages and ask that folks in the area come out and observe, take notes and get the names and badge numbers of the violators. You can also use twitter, Facebook and some of the other social networks but you may put yourself at risk by openly stopping their progress opposed to the more clandestine text alert. Institute Operation Cop Block today!

Sounding the Akoben (War Horn)

For a few decades, the liberation movement seemed to be comatose or dead and in need of either, some form of cardiopulmonary resuscitation or a full resurrection. Since the uprisings of the 60's there has not been any serious rush of mass organizing in regards to the Black Liberation Struggle here in the U.S. There have been plenty of mobilizations and a few rebellions, but nothing that has kept the people in revolutionary thought and action mode. One thing is for certain; no matter how "sick and tired of being sick and tired" our people have been, Stolen Afrikans in America have always had some form of supernatural Novocain to not necessarily cure the mental affliction but to ease the discomfort to a point that they forget the illness exists, until of course the numbness subsides. One of the chief anesthesiologists going back to slavery here in America has been the preacher and the black church. Of course we know the church has served and continues to serve as a place of refuge and as a meeting hub to organize for many of our people. No one can deny that. Certainly, it was used more effectively for liberation purposes at the height of our physical bondage in this country. Along with the preacher and the church, it was also those old Negro spirituals, the hymns that kept us inebriated and elated. The luminous rhythms that radiated through the powerful voices much like the melanin of the Stolen Afrikans (along with the keys of the piano) electrified "the people of the book" so much so that they felt it in their souls, causing them to "catch the holy ghost". It was this ol' time religion that helped to carry our ancestors thru their trials and tribulations. On the plantation, the hymnals were used by the slaves crooning in the field to aid in passing the time away as they toiled from dusk to dawn. In many cases these same melodies were used as valuable communiqués that broadcast a soundtrack to revolt. It was the preacher and the church being used as a practical, not abstract tool for liberation that would give birth to the likes of David Walker, Nat Turner, Denmark Vesey, Boukman, Dessalines, Paul Bogle and countless others. Later on, the chain gangs and road crews that labored and continue to labor under the New Jim Crow would carry on the tradition.

Ascension to Soul Rhapsody

Our people have always operated off of an extended heartbeat in the form of art, music and dance that has kept them in harmony with the universe. That extended heartbeat has sustained and been somewhat of a savior to a suffering culture often threatened with extinction. Throughout the 20th Century our people have taken the art form of music to heights unimaginable. From Jazz to Blues, Rock n Roll to Hip Hop, our people have delivered messages of resistance and what some would say defiance that has served as a backdrop for our struggle. Cultural workers like Paul Robeson the strong, bold actor/singer/activist of international appeal took the message of our struggle and oppression global. Thru his vocal opposition to U.S. policy he became an enemy of the state so much so that he was white-balled in this country and was poisoned by the CIA while in Russia. I remember listening to a tape of Malcolm X and he talked about how while he served time in prison he would listen to Paul Robeson faithfully and that he had actually adopted his speaking style from Robeson. An example of art reaching beyond entertainment or art for art sake.

Without going into the history of 20th Century sounds of resistance, I can say that there have been many socially and politically charged soul school vocalists that have inspired me. Artists such as Billie Holiday, Nina Simone, James Brown, Marvin Gaye, The Last Poets, Gil Scot-Heron and Curtis Mayfield. And when we talk about artists of my time, those from the Hip Hop culture have certainly played a role in my organizing efforts, both as an individual and as a representative of an organization. In fact, Public Enemy, NWA and X-Clan indirectly aided in the naming of The FTP Movement thru some of their music. Public Enemy with "Fight the Power", NWA with "Fuck the Police" and X-Clan with "FTP". It was a combination of their cultural strategy and the politics that I acquired while gritting my teeth in struggle that to a great extent has helped us to attract countless people from my generation and under.

Professor Griff, Kalonji, Wise Intelligent, Min Server,
Uno The Prophet at 4th of U-Lie Event

Atlanta Ambassador making an effort to stop FTP
Movement from feeding the people. He approached FTP
in a rude manner and Bro. Vision teaches him a lesson
in proper etiquette.

Justice for Troy Davis during Martin Luther King Day March. Taj Anwar, Bro. Damu, Eboni Joy, Kalonji

Dalani, Kalonji, Sengor Bey, Professor Kamau Kambon

KRS-1, Kalonji meets at Criminal Records

FTP Movement representing Political Prisoners at Annual King March

Black August Commemoration Concert
Karen Marie Mason, Kalonji, Paradise Gray of X-Clan,
Ras Kofi, Killer Mike, Minister Server, Jasiri X

Iffat Muhammad, Damu, The Late- Billy McKinney, John Evans of Operation Lead, Kalonji Changa and Congresswoman Cynthia McKinney at the home Kathryn Johnston, the 92 year old shot down by Atlanta Police in her own home...We will never forget!

Young Kalonji Changa preparing for his future assignments.

FTP Weekend in Los Angeles, CA with local FTP Chapter marked the merger of FTP Movement and the Black August Organizing Committee.

FTP Weekend in Atlanta, GA with local FTP Chapter and Supporters

Creative Loafing cover story featuring Food, Clothing, Shelter CD. Front Row- Rita J, Senor Kaos, Mike Flo Second Row- Boog Brown, Kalonji, Taj Anwar, Stahhr, The DollDaze, Khalilah Ali Third Row- Ekundayo, Amond Jackson, Chosen, Kelly Love Jones & the babies.

Feed The People program circa. 2004, Chairman Fred Hampton, Jr. of the POCC, Kalonji, and FTP Supporters

Professor Griff, Kalonji, Bro J of X-Clan

FTP Siafu- Peaches serving the people.

Kalonji, Precise Science (Hip- Hop Group) and Dhoruba
Bin Wahad sharing a laugh at Kalonji's expense.

From Rage City to Serving the People

As a young Hip Hop artist, in 1986 I was offered a record deal with an independent label. Gung ho about being presented a recording contract, like many other gullible ghetto youth in pursuit of a way out via a talent that they ardently adored, I signed what I later discovered was one of the most rinky-dink agreements on the planet. 5 years later, after recuperating from my blunder and wanting to spare others the sweet taste of chocolate cyanide, I partnered with a friend; Terry Bowman and we formed an entertainment company called Rage City Records. Half-artist, half-label owner I utilized Rage City as a launch pad to thrust my ideology into the hearts and minds of all who I came in contact with. Rage City was more than an independent label; it was a marketing & promotions agency, a fledgling consultation firm and more importantly a statement. It was a statement because it was 1991 and you had two young black males (I was 21 at the time and Terry was a few years older) that were making an effort to pave their way as an independent music group thru uncharted territory in the small inner city of Bridgeport, Connecticut. We made our public debut by being featured on the front page and centerfold of the Sunday edition of the Connecticut Post, the most widely read paper in the city and the state. It seemed like everybody and they mama literally, saw that issue, all of a sudden it was like we were the Russell Simmons' of the ghetto-minus the dough. Knowing that we had to seize the time in order to maintain our relevance, and get money, we began to promote local talent shows and what we called the "Tri-State Talent Blast" an event that attracted artists, labels and fans from New York, New Jersey and Connecticut. During that time we attracted then unknowns, such as Sean "Puffy" Coombs, Brian McKnight and Cypress Hill to name a few. Soon after, I began promoting club events. I was so confident with my skills that I began promoting two clubs on the same night and at the same time, one block over from each other. I was running a college night at a club called *Living Color* and an R&B night at another club called *The Essence* and they were both successful. After a few years of pushing the Rage City ticket, I discovered that promotions was my forte and that I needed to spread my wings and fly into bigger arenas. By 1993, we parked the Rage City car and I propelled a new entity called "The Ill Mob World Hip Hop League". For the next 6 years, through the Ill Mob, I ventured out to booking and management to accompany the marketing & promotions services I previously delivered. During that period my clientele included artists from labels such as Profile, Def Jam, Arista, Tommy Boy and Blunt Records to name a few.

By the year 1999, after over a decade of working within the entertainment industry, marketing, promoting, and managing artists; that particular field had taken such a toll on me that I didn't want any parts of it. All the late nights, weed, liquor and day-to-day hustle were not worth the unnecessary stress. All I wanted to do was work on behalf of my people and I felt that the music business was the antitheses of working for the people. I decided I had to make a choice between getting a check for helping to destroy lives (including my own) or committing myself to doing what I knew all my life was right, serving the people.

Black is Back

During the late eighties and early nineties there was a serious upsurge of "conscious music". We had folks like Public Enemy, X-Clan, Boogie Down Productions, Queen Latifah, Brand Nubian, Tupac Shakur, Lakim Shabazz and a host of others. With these artists, along with filmmaker Spike Lee's screen version of *Malcolm X*, it was once again

102

"cool" for the masses to display their Afrikan Pride. It was a common thing and somewhat of a trend to see Afrikan medallions, cars riding by bumpin' rebel music, "X" hats and jackets, and all types of paraphernalia indicative of Black culture. Unfortunately, the longevity of a fad is more often than not a short-lived epoch. As quickly as this era was ushered in, the industry put dollars and power behind entertaining distractions and that period eventually fizzled out. It wasn't until around 2000 when I was first introduced to the music of my comrades, dead prez that it seemed that the youth still stood a chance.

I was first introduced to the music of dead prez in 2000 when I was a partner in a Black owned cultural hemp shop in Bridgeport. We were positioned inside of a downtown strip mall and inside the strip mall there were a small number of independently owned businesses mainly geared towards inner-city residents. There was a tattoo shop, a few clothing shops and a Hip-Hop music store owned and operated by my homie Kingsley, a popular Dj/promoter from the Continent. It was Kingsley who gave me a Styrofoam VHS promo of a group called "dead prez". I actually had the video which was for the song, "Bigger than Hip Hop" sitting next to one of the televisions we had in the store for about 3 months before I even popped in it. On the TV we usually played lectures such as Malcolm, Dr. John Henrik Clarke, Dr. Ben, Marimba Ani, old Panther footage etc., so I had no reason to play this Styrofoam promo. One day out of the blue I decided to pop the video in while I was assisting a customer, thinking it was a group of country rappers, I paid it no mind. The video had played and went off and I was working on something else, until my partner Sulaiman came in and noticed the blue screen and decided to rewind the tape. He watched it and was like "Oh shit! Who are these dudes", I replied, "I don't know and I didn't even listen to that bullshit". So he got me to check it out. I viewed it and I immediately walked across the hall and purchased the cd and it played in the store non-stop for damn near a week straight. At the time we were organizing under the banner of "The Universal Black Panther Party" and the cd *Let's get free* was our modern "soundtrack to the revolution" and it was obligatory for every member to have a copy. My respect for the group grew further when I attended the International African Arts Festival in Brooklyn and bumped into group member M1, who was not on stage rappin' but selling *Burning Spear* newspapers for the Uhuru Movement. I can honestly say that it was that encounter along with the inspiration from some of the earlier revolutionary artists that got my wheels turning about starting a Hip Hop group for the sole purpose of organizing the masses. The group became known as "FTP" and it was actually a duo consisting of a Sista who went by "Z" (Zakiyah Muhammad) and "The Riot Starter" (myself). In all honestly, the group never really got off the ground the way we intended but, I continued to do shows (spoken word) as "The Riot Starter from the Revolutionary Hip Hop group FTP", just to keep the FTP concept alive. At the same time, I had linked up with Chairman Fred Hampton Jr. and joined The Prisoners of Conscience Committee (POCC) and was named the Chief Coordinator of the organization. As fate would have it, I ended up serving on the board with both members of the group dead prez. M1 was the Minister of Culture and Sticman served as the Minister of Health along with other great activists including my brother Nkrumah Anpu who was the Field Marshall, Marcus Kline (Frontline Magazine) was the Minister of Education, Kamel Bell (son of Political Prisoner Herman Bell) Chief of Staff, JR (from the SF Bayview) the Minister of Information and a host of other dynamic organizers.

Hip Hop University

Recognizing the power of Hip Hop, in 2003, I landed a position as a teacher at Windham Academy, an alternative high school in Willimantic, Connecticut. The school was comprised of a predominately African/Latino student populace that numbered about 95% in comparison to an approximate 5% poor white student body. Windham Academy was designed to teach "troubled" students who couldn't handle public school (or rather public school couldn't handle them). Really to me, it had all the ingredients of an average low-income inner-city school. Teenage pregnancies, substance abuse, sexual abuse, hunger, homelessness and over half the students were from foster homes, had been arrested and were under state supervision. Everything a child's nightmare is made of. The vast majority of the students had poor attendance and there was a serious drop out rate. At first glance their situation appeared bleak and their future seemed hopeless but from an organizer's perspective it was right down my alley. Always pro-underdog and a lover of the unloved, I was convinced from day one that I could make an impact and change the game. I knew I had to teach these youth, help build their self-esteem, prepare them for real life, and provide conflict resolution, which was foreseeable due to the multiple personalities and shared pain, which was being channeled in the form of misguided aggression and detestation. A gargantuan task ahead, I knew that before I could began to implement any ideas or thoughts I has to first win the students over and get them to trust me. I knew I had to understand before being understood. In observing them I realized that a major portion of the pupils had some type of talent related to the arts so I felt that if they were able to express themselves thru art, we may possibly produce better results. Mind you, thanks to the government the Clinton and Bush administrations did away with a large number of arts programs in the school system particularly in the underprivileged communities and of course this school was amongst the victims. There were no programs at all.

I began to talk to the students about my background in the music business, did a little name-droppin' to peak their interest and bam-a-lam! I got their attention. At that point I found that there were more hidden talents than I detected. For the next few days, the main topic of discussion was my experience in the music business. I decided to broker a deal with them, come to school (on time), do what I require of you and I will assist, advice and aid you in showcasing your talents. They were wide open. Seeing their enthusiasm and not wanting to be the next person to let them down, I began to think of ways to assist them in honing and displaying their skills. I noticed that inside of the school, there was an old auditorium that wasn't really being utilized for anything other than in-school suspension and boring ass meetings. So the idea came to me to help the students produce a talent show, which would be called "The One Mic Stand", a play on of sort to a one-night stand. A few days later I stopped by the principal's office ran the idea pass him and he was elated. Cool I thought, and then the work began. From Jump Street, my goal was to educate, organize and politicize the youth by any means, so in order to do that I knew I had to visualize the project from beginning to end to bring it into manifestation. I had to get all the youth involved with this project, whether they were artists or not. In formatting the event, I had the students list every position that they knew was involved in the production of a talent show, concert or any similar type of program. Everyone had a role to play; some students were stage managers, ushers, production assistants, front desk clerks and cashiers. The students who were known as the "toughest" or the most unruly were the ones that were given the security positions because I knew that they would help to enforce the rules and regulations with the other students. I invited some of my people from the music business down to participate as judges and the event was a big success. The principal invited members of the all-white Board of Education to the show and they raved over the "trouble teens" that they had previously written off. The following day the principal called me into his office super excited telling me how the Board loved the event, he loved it and that we had to do more of it. That's when I hit him with *Hip Hop University Cultural Initiative* a program that I had developed to teach the youth thru Hip Hop and to encourage them to stay in school. A week later, I was sitting in front of the Windham County Board of Education discussing implementing HHU into Windham Academy's curriculum. I was offered $30 an hour as Director of Hip Hop University with a budget of $30,000 a year to purchase whatever materials were needed to ensure the best results of the project.

One of the most valuable lessons I learned about organizing on any capacity is to not deal in absolutes, to meet people where they are and to make sure that they are put in positions to do things they either naturally do or have a desire or passion for. Along with a budget for the program, I was given two classrooms, one large open space and one small area. In the bigger class I wanted to make it a cool, hip atmosphere (almost like a coffee shop) so instead of chairs like a traditional classroom, I had leather couches installed, the walls were lined up with posters of Bob Marley, Tupac, Erykah Badu and a few others. I had a bookshelf with Music Business 101 books, Source Magazines, Vibe Magazines and any other Black music related publication I could find. We also had a television with a shelf full of every Hip Hop related dvd available at the time, including Beat Street, Wild Style, Breakin', Krush Groove and several others.

In the second classroom I had a fully equipped soundproof pro-tools studio built, so that the students could produce and record their own demos. We also had 3 mini dv cameras that were used to record their own videos, which were eventually used to land them a public access television show. With this arsenal, I had their full cooperation. Every child in the school was a part of this program. The only requirements to utilize the equipment, and to move beyond the theory to the practical were to come to school (on time), maintain their discipline and to get good grades in all of their classes. It worked, the kids came to school everyday (some would be in my classroom before I got there), their grades increased and together we made school inspirational and educational. The cool thing about this situation was that I was the only person qualified to teach about the music business and the history of Hip Hop, so besides the principal (who trusted my guidance and didn't bother me) I was my immediate supervisor.

As organizers, we understand the first onus upon us is to fight ignorance. So with the students I utilized Hip Hop University not just as a means to entertain, inspire or teach them in the orthodox American way but to politicize them on the reality of the world and the oppressive system that had played a major role in the placing of the stumbling blocks and obstacles that they faced. I had to teach them to use every obstacle as a stepping-stone, just as the ants do. I began to politicize the students thru music first by breaking down song lyrics. I would have them listen to music by Tupac, Public Enemy, dead prez, The Coup, Rage Against the Machine, The Welfare Poets, The Last Poets, Gil Scot-Heron, Curtis Mayfield and many others. Through the socially conscious tunes, I was able to segue into information about revolutionaries, human rights, self worth, and the effects of capitalism, slavery, Jim Crow and the power of the people. I made it cool to have knowledge of our struggle and to get involved in it. I gave the students the task of depositing what they were acquiring into their art and it worked. The program proved successful! It was so successful that by the end of the year I was informed by the Board of Education that the budget to pay me for my work had to be eliminated for the next school year. It was disappointing but at the same time it was encouraging because I completed my mission by providing a foundation for the students to grow from and at the same time I got paid by the system to teach our next generation to holistically oppose that which is diametrically opposed to them.

Hip Hop Politricks

During the nineties, political figures and community leaders such as Rev. Calvin O. Butts III, pastor of the Abyssinian Baptist Church in Harlem and politician/civil rights activist C. Delores Tucker held major crusades against "gangsta rap" and explicit lyrics, literally taking Hip Hop tapes and steamrolling them in front of the world. Almost two decades later, everyone from major corporations such as McDonalds to IBM to politicians such as Al Sharpton and Barack Obama have utilized Hip Hop as a means of selling bullshit to the people. In 2004, Hip Hop moguls, Sean "Puffy" Combs and Russell Simmons pimped Hip Hop by pushing the *"Vote or Die"* Campaign which was used as a means to put themselves in a position to gain political clout. They used the artist to push their agenda and further establish Hip Hop as a bargaining chip to influence the masses to support the elite. The end results were their clothing companies, *Sean John* and *Phat Farm* made millions of dollars off of Vote or Die t-shirts, they played both sides of the fence with the Democratic and Republican parties, Puffy went on tour with Hillary Clinton, and Hip Hop was proven to have muscle in regards to swaying the vote towards the desired results. The people voted and are still going to die.

In 2005, after Hurricane Katrina hit New Orleans and George Bush flew pass the victims, rapper Kanye West made the statement "George Bush don't care about Black people" on live television. Much of White America was outraged, because they knew it was true but were in denial because a descendant of slaves had the audacity to publicly utter those words after accepting fame and trinkets from them. George Bush was so infuriated that even after his presidency was up (five years after the incident), during an interview with NBC's Matt Lauer he stated that Kanye's statement was "the lowest point of his presidency". Ain't that a bitch!

Fast forward to 2010, the day after the massive tragic earthquake hit Haiti the first public figure to "come to the rescue" was rapper Wyclef Jean asking people around the world to text donations via cell phone to his organization Yéle. At first glance the average person thought it was an honorable way for the artist to support his homeland until it was discovered that him and his uncle Raymond Joseph were amongst those who supported the coup that forced former Haiti President Aristide into exile. With the people suffering from the earthquake catastrophe, it was a perfect time to run the U.S. based Hip Hop artist for president of Haiti. Later on Jean may have realized that the people don't play, when a bullet grazed his hand while visiting the historic island.

We know that Hip Hop played a major role in Barack Obama's election with folks like Jay Z, Young Jeezy and Will-i-am co-signing for him with songs, videos and shout outs. The best tribute that I saw was Aaron McGrudders' cartoon depiction of rapper Will-i-am performing a song called "d*ck ridin Obama". Will-i-am wasn't happy about it but, it sure as hell tickled me. Even our Brother Common who shed light amongst Hip Hoppers` internationally with his "Song for Assatta", a dope piece that some folks would say was their introduction to the Movement, drank the Kool-Aid. After it was announced that Common was invited to perform at the White House, everyone from Sarah Palin to the Tea Party denounced his music, saying that he had "cop killer lyrics". During the May 2011 performance at the White House, Common was quoted as saying, ""Politics is politics and everyone is entitled to their own opinion, I respect that. The one thing that shouldn't be questioned is my support for the police officers and troops that protect us every day". How he went from Assatta to entertaining the thought of supporting the police is insanity at its best. The same thing I told KRS One, I will say to Common, "As an artist you are one of the best but as far as your politics and philosophies, I can't fuck with you".

Hip Hop as a tool to organize the community

"The role of the artist is as important as the role of the guerrilla" –Che Guevara

In the second decade of the 21st century, I think that most organizers that have the ability to reach the youth, whether it's un-politicized brothers and sisters or those who have a yearning to be equipped with the knowledge to aid in the advancement and liberation of our people would agree that Hip Hop can be used as a tool to organize the community. I am a firm believer in what you don't control, will eventually control you. Hip Hop has gone through various stages but for the organizer it is imperative that we use whatever tool necessary to complete our mission. I would say that The FTP Movement has mastered the art of using the phenomenon of the day to reach not only the youth but also the masses to accomplish goals and to educate while in the process. We use the voice and imagery of the artist because we know that a message with a beat or a visual picture will be seen and projected with more of an impact and a magnitude than just the average person on a

111

soap box. Around the globe we have utilized the artist to organize on all levels. Many organizations only work with "conscious artist"; I like to work with any serious artist that is willing to connect around points of unity. I usually make an effort to reach for the apolitical artist because in many cases they have a broader base and have the attention of the masses. By dealing with the apolitical artist it's a dual educational process, the artist is learning and providing unchartered territory to introduce our message and propaganda. We utilize the skills of the visual artist to enhance the imagery and make the packages more appealing. Whether its through flyers, posters, videos, web design or photos we make every effort to make it hip to organize, it is important that the people know that "organizing is the new cool". Oftentimes you will find community workers making an effort to remix the 60's instead of paving their own way. They get stuck on old school styles and wonder why they can't reach a new school audience. I hear organizers talk about "the people ain't ready" and "our folks are not interested in the plight of the people". The people only know what they see and in many cases they see the same old tired, dry strategies and tactics. By no means am I saying abandon what our Elders and Ancestors taught, I am saying that you have to be in tune with the times and meet people where they are. There are tons of new and innovative ways to get our message across by using bright, vivid and glaring visuals that speak a language that the people want to hear. The FTP Movement developed an artist collective made of independent artist that are not viewed as traditional freedom fighters but mainly supporters of the campaigns and programs that we provide. I would be remiss to overlook the fact that these creative individuals who have gradually advance to cultural workers are one of the key components and main ingredients to the success rate of our movement. From the branding of the logos to the event production they have helped to catapult our programs and position internationally. I have found myself being interviewed by magazines and radio stations from places like Jamaica, Japan, Italy, France, Russia and numerous places on the continent, which can all be attributed to the work I do as a freedom fighter utilizing Hip Hop as a tool to organize the community.

Below I have listed a few examples of some of the projects, programs and events we do or have done in which the artist role is tantamount to that of the revolutionary.

Food, Clothes & Shelter: *The Street Album-*A 44 track double disc cd in which various mainly underground artist/supporters from around the country submitted some of the hottest material created. This project was put together for the sole purpose of supporting political prisoners and our feed the people program. The beautiful thing about this project is that it is reality based and produced by the people for the people. While every song is not a "revolutionary track", it is great music. I run into folks all the time that make "conscious music" with positive lyrics but it sounds awful. Then they get upset with the people for not supporting it. That's like because I'm a vegetarian I should eat whatever food is nutritional even if it doesn't taste good. We have to make sure what we give the people is palatable and they will come back for more.

Poets 4 Political Prisoners- In an effort to educate the masses about the plight of African and colonized warriors who have been kidnapped and held for ransom, we launched Poets 4 Political Prisoners. Poets 4 Political Prisoners is a tool used to educate through the use of poetry

113

and hip- hop, highlighting freedom fighters and activists. Poets 4 Political Prisoners also serves as a benefit to support the creation of materials such as, CD's and newspapers that will be used for comrade's legal expenses and commissary. Past participants include: Amiri Baraka, Amir Sulaiman, Fred Hampton Jr., Mukasa Dada, Bilal Sunni-Ali, Georgia Me, Abyss, Queen Sheba, Askia Toure, Sunni Patterson and a host of others.

FTP Movement Artist Collective- As mentioned above, FTP knows the power of the microphone and the importance of visual appeal. We understand that a message can be conveyed and internalized more effectively through a song, video or other means of visual arts, than through a speech or lecture. With that in mind we developed the FTP Movement Artist Collective. Minister Huey P. Newton of the Black Panther Party said, "Power is the ability to define phenomena and make it act in a desired manner". The FTP Movement Artist Collective utilizes the cultural phenomenon of Hip Hop to work in the interest of the people through education, fundraisers, etc. We don't just recruit the so-called "conscious rapper"; we work with anyone that can unite around issues that affect us. Not limited to Hip Hop, the Artist Collective is comprised of poets, singers, graphic designers, actors and other cultural workers internationally. The artists educate the masses through the production of CD's, DVD's, videos, events & other means of communication. Currently the FTP Artist Collective is working on a national marketing and promotions team armed with an independent distribution network.

Crew Love- is a concert showcase series in which independent artist from different regions lend their time and talents to aid in bringing community concern back to Hip

Hop. Each Crew Love focuses on different topics or social ills to provide awareness and insight in an effort to motivate the audience. Different dj's and emcees add a unique flavor that infuses good music with pertinent information that captivates, edutains and inspires the observer. Past Crew Loves have been dedicated to victims of police terrorism, political prisoners and homelessness. The proceeds raised by the events benefit the various programs we deliver.

Present Date In Time

Everybody's trying to be politically correct
revamped ghetto terminology to "urban"
with hopes of reversing the negative effects
of neighborhoods producing hoods
and if our mind's eye weren't blinded by cream
we'd willingly acknowledge our responsibility
take the time to refine the drug game's boldest
into educated soldiers holding down corners
saving lives granting sight to the blind

Yet instead...most of us are mentally dead
black masses satisfied with month-2-month rentals
no insurance for meds nor dental project pads decked out
by mo'fo's with no financial clout low-class family can barely eat
still momma rocks Gucci head-2-feet dries her ass with Tommy's towels
gets her freak on in Veronica's nightgowns inebriated day or night all around town
while her ig'nant child runs wild and we have the nerve to wonder how
the "white oppressor" keeps us down

NIGGA PLEASE

it ain't him... it's us too lazy to make a fuss
get on the bus and raise a ruckus
believing luck is going to save those
lacking in initiative making kids
to get paid off public assistance
and like a fool you put up a personal resistance to view the
news

WARNING-public aid is ending soon
and affirmative action too disbelievers acting coy
when told social security's becoming null and void
falling victim to the ploys of those
who used to blast us with their water hose
burn us live and save the bones as trophies
infested our communities with keys of her'on and crack-
coke
U.S. government the only one got permanently rich off
selling dope

And so...
we no longer think alike...speak alike...
or see alike...
We've been grafted like their kind
through the poisoning of our mind's with swine
built this country off our Black behinds
and at age 225 we still provide the cheapest labor
get locked-up and you're doing them a favor
and there'll be no Captain Save'em Ho to get yo ass
released
and those who're physically free...
you're still captive in the streets
through mental bondage

-Eboni Joy

The Obama-nation Abomination

"Democrats or republican- just two sides of the same coin, either way it's still white power. It's the same system, just changed forms ". –dead prez (Politrikkks)

I recently asked a group of individuals who is the enemy in which we should be fighting against. The answers ranged from imperialism, capitalism, Zionism, colonialism to white supremacy. I got to admit the number one answer was global white supremacy. Of course white folks have undeniably been the cause of more destruction and death on this planet than any other group of people. This is an irrefutable fact that cannot be disputed on any level. Whether you call it global white supremacy, white domination or its notorious by-product and shining forerunner capitalism it's all part of the same family. Now is this a racist statement? Is it biased? Study history and as El Hajj Malik El Shabazz (Malcolm X) stated, "History is best qualified to reward all research". Am I saying that all white people are bad? No, I am not saying that either. That would be like saying all Black folks are good. I will however say that based on my research, experience and interactions with white folks that they are certainly a soulless people and my statement is proven by their ways and actions. I would even dare to go a step further and say that when it comes to white domination that it transcends the color lines. Our Brother H. Rap Brown would say, "To be Black is necessary, but it's not sufficient". In other words before a cow is slaughtered the cow is made comfortable. The cow is fed well and taken care of, all in preparation for the slaughter. The cow becomes so relaxed that it is actually clueless to the process of its own elimination. So much so that when it is time to be slaughtered, the cow never knew what hit her. That's how it is in America, because a Black face is paraded in front of the "African-American", in certain instances our people become tranquil.

Kwame Nkrumah said, "Neo-colonialism is the last stage of imperialism". While still reeking of the same stench, what happened on November 4th, 2008 was not neo-colonialism, but certainly marked a new era of democratic fascism, where people voluntarily surrender whatever so-called freedom they still possessed. Now we have oppressed Black folks, who secretly love their oppressor, and want so badly to be part of the oppressors politics (even though they have no clear understanding of it), for the sake of their race being recognized as a viable force, rooting for a charming Black mask on a ruthless white face. When it comes to European style politics a persons race has never played a part in the advancement of the poor and oppressed. A representative of the oppressor can do nothing but just that- represent the oppressor and no one can deny that. It's unfortunate that many of our Brothers and Sisters have been duped into believing that the 'change' Barack Obama spoke of was for the betterment of Black People. The smooth orator that he is, equipped with the slick sound bites and a brilliantly delivered array of speeches, Mr. Obama has not and will not address the issues that affect Black people. The first time he spoke in regards to police brutality he did not side with justice, he sided with the law. Even though the blind fold on the lady of justice, prevents her from seeing that the law is imbalanced. During a press conference held at a gas station in Indianapolis, Obama was asked about the acquittal of the New York detectives who murdered Sean Bell and he responded by saying, "the judge has made his ruling, and we're a nation of laws, so we respect the verdict that came down". So in a nutshell, so what if 50 shots were fired at unarmed civilians, who broke no law, other than driving while Black, what did the judge say? The next time we heard from your President regarding police misconduct was when his good friend Henry Louis "Skip" Gates was arrested for charges that stemmed from allegedly breaking into his own home. Skip Gates a Black man, who is a recognized author and Harvard Professor, who in 1997 was named one of the 25 most influential Americans by Time Magazine, was arrested at his home in Cambridge, Massachusetts after police responded to a possible break in. Skip who had just returned home from China, had trouble getting into his front door, so he forced his way in. According to reports, Cambridge police Sergeant James Crowley arrived on the scene, Mr. Gates produced identification and other proof that he was the owner of the home, and was asked to step outside, at which time he refused. A verbal altercation ensued and Gates was arrested. During a press conference, Barack Obama commented that, "The police are doing what they should. There's a call and they go investigate. What happens? My understanding is that Professor Gates then shows his ID to prove that this is his house, and at that point he gets arrested for disorderly conduct." He went on to say that Cambridge police acted "stupidly" in arresting somebody when there was already proof that they were in their own home. He also stated, "Separate and apart from this incident, there is a long history in this country of African-Americans and Latinos being stopped by police disproportionately. That's just a fact." Now all that sounded great, until next thing you know, in an attempt to not lose popularity with white America and to not upset the Fraternal Order of Police and others- Mr. Obama invites Professor Gates, Sergeant Crowley and Vice President Joe Biden to join him for a beer summit at the White House. So while the Oscar Grants, Kathryn Johnstons and 7-year-old Aiyana Joneses are being murdered by police in America, the President, Vice President, the police and the prestigious professor are chugging down brews in the White House!

Seems like old times. The perfect time to deal with police terrorism and once again your president proves who he's rollin' with.

When asked about the issue of reparations, he stated, "the best reparations we can provide are good schools in the inner city and jobs for people who are unemployed". What does that have to do with reparations? In any civilized society a quality education and the basic necessities; food, clothing and shelter go without saying. The $600 million + dollars, spent on Barack's campaign could have been used for the "good schools and jobs for people who are unemployed". Obama would have never made a statement like that to Israel. Israel receives $1.8 billion in military aid and $1.2 billion in economic aid from the United States yearly, as reparations for the "Jewish Holocaust". Yet, when it comes to the atrocities committed against African people, the mere thought is quickly dismissed. In fact Barack has already pledged his allegiance to the Zionist state of Israel. The day after his democratic nomination he made the statement, that "any enemy of Israel is an enemy of the United States", and after the election the first person appointed, was his then Chief of Staff, Rahm Israel Emmanuel, a known Zionist.

For some strange reason, Black folks, who Obama has not shown any allegiance, seem to be under a spell, in their belief that suddenly, Barack Obama because of his skin color is going to fight on their behalf. Believing that is like saying a police officer won't mistreat you if he has a vegan diet and occasionally wears Afrikan garb. Mr. Obama never once stated that he was working toward the advancement of Black people; he said he was working for change for Americans. America does not and has never in any capacity, worked in our interest; historically it has always worked toward our demise. America has kidnapped us, raped us, enslaved us, experimented on us, put drugs and guns into our communities and outright murdered us. Now suddenly, with the flick of a switch, and the backing of corporate America and Wall Street investment banks, we have a Black president; reared by white relatives in Hawaii, a graduate of Harvard University that can truly relate to the plight of Black America? In what way can he relate? Is it because he has a Black wife, and Black children? Or is it because he plays basketball?

It saddens me to see so many of our people from the so-called "conscious community" who drank the Kool-Aid. The number of phone calls and e-mails I received regarding "our Black president" was frightening. The first call I received was from a Sistah, who for all practical purposes is respected in the black community. She said that she was calling to congratulate me on "Our new president", thinking she was joking, I said, "You mean your president?" she responded by saying, "I see you still on that black stuff". Amazingly, after all this time, we still haven't recognized that the enemy will use those who look most like us, to defeat us. For years, Black America has been primed for this occasion, fattened for the slaughter. They gave us Black police officers, Black mayors, Black governors, Black judges, Black generals etc.... How soon we forget that Colin Powell is Black. Condoleza Rice is Black and so is Clarence Thomas, Black by popular demand. In 1985, it was the first Black mayor of Philadelphia, Wilson Goode who ordered police to bomb a house on Osage Avenue occupied by members of the MOVE family, killing men, women and children. It was Black cops who assisted in the murders and cover-ups of Fred Hampton, Mark Clark, Sean Bell and 92-year-old Kathryn Johnston. So again, to be Black is necessary, but it's not sufficient.

Some may still think Barack, the charismatic brother that he is, may change things. The fact remains that even if he wanted to change the conditions of Black people, he has a job description, and he has to stick to the script. In that job description, he oversees a corrupt, criminal enterprise built from the domination, destruction and death of innocent people. Now, he may be a "good guy", I don't know him personally, but I do know if you are a chef and you get a job at McDonalds, just because you like to cook blackened steak, lobster bisque and cordon bleu, that's not what's on the menu at McDonalds. At McDonalds, it's Big Macs, Happy Meals and Quarter Pounders. You have to stick to the menu and our liberation is not on America's menu and the moment Obama strays away and wants to go off course, there will be another JFK grassy knoll incident.

Out of fear, you have a few certified and government approved, self-appointed, imitation nationalist, the wolves in sheep's clothes, who have remixed the "Change gone come" song to sell to their gullible flock. These scared to death Negroes who, would rather switch than fight. 'Political Punks' as Dhoruba would say. They purposefully, mislead people when they know the truth. When it comes to this government Blacks are like battered wives, they have been abused so long that they believe it's out of love. So now, with Barack, I guess its Black Love. Our people are so hungry, in search of hope, that they will eat anything that appears edible. Now don't get me wrong, I am not a hater. It's a beautiful thing to see a Black Family appear to be in charge; however, I am a realist and I know that the reality in any puppet show is that there are always strings attached. The state pulled a number on us with the Bush regime, so after 8 years of Bush, the dream of 'Change' sounds, oh so good. So here comes your tall, dark and handsome, knight in shining armor, to fulfill your dreams. With that I will say, time will tell, and I will also quote another legendary "Black Man", Flava Flav and say, "Don't believe the hype". To many of our people, this election marked the beginning of hope; to students of history it marks the continuation of global white supremacy. Anytime a president, a Black man sends 30,000 troops to occupy another country and 10 days later he receives the Nobel Peace Prize you better believe that the dice are loaded and the deck is stacked.

COINTELPRO: The Destruction of a Movement

"The Negro youth and moderates must be made to understand that if they succumb to revolutionary teaching, they will be dead revolutionaries." -Communiqué sent April 3, 1968 by San Francisco FBI Field Office to FBI Director J. Edgar Hoover (It should be noted that one day later Dr. Martin Luther King Jr. was assassinated in Memphis)

As the struggle for our liberation intensifies, we must lock and load, set the scope and aim at one of the arch-nemesis of the people, the infamous COINTELPRO. Orchestrated by the late sinister J. Edgar Hoover and carried out by the FBI, COINTELPRO (counterintelligence program) was launched for all intent and purposes to (in their words) "expose, disrupt, misdirect, discredit, or otherwise neutralize the activities of black nationalist, hate-type organizations and groupings, their leadership, spokesmen, membership, and supporters, and to counter their propensity for violence and civil disorder." On March 8, 1971, a group known as the Citizens' Commission to Investigate the FBI broke into an FBI office in Media, Pennsylvania and liberated thousands of files that outlined and documented the vast illegal operation known as COINTELPRO. The group then disseminated the information to various media outlets throughout the globe. The COINTELPRO papers blew the lid off of the criminal counterinsurgency program that was launched in 1956. From 1956 throughout the 70's, the FBI, under the direction of the demented, bitter Mr. Hoover, assassinated the character, mental and physical bodies of organizations such as SNCC (Student Non-violent Coordinating Committee), RNA (Republic of New Africa), RAM

(Revolutionary Action Movement), AIM (American Indian Movement) and the Black Panther Party to name a few. The FBI also kept dossiers on everyone from Malcolm X and Martin Luther King Jr. to Dick Gregory, Richard Pryor and anyone else that could influence the people. It is safe to say that during the 60's COINTELPRO was the cause of the majority of the rifts, assassinations and imprisonment of civil and human rights activist of that time. In fact, the use of infiltrators, agent provocateurs and snitches were used in every serious organization of that era. From the issues between the Nation of Islam and Malcolm X, the original east coast-west coast beef between the Black Panther Party to the assassinations of Martin Luther King, and Fred Hampton-Black agents were used to infiltrate and to aid Counterinsurgency program in the destruction of our own. The following excerpts were part of the documents seized during the Media, PA office raid:

Intensified attention under this program should be afforded to the activities of such groups as the Student Nonviolent Coordinating Committee, the Southern Christian Leadership Conference, Revolutionary Action Movement, the Deacons for Defense and Justice, Congress of Racial Equality, and the Nation of Islam. Particular emphasis should be given to extremists who direct the activities and policies of revolutionary or militant groups such as Stokely Carmichael, H. "Rap" Brown, Elijah Muhammad, and Maxwell Stanford. Director to 23 Field Offices, Aug. 26, 1967

The Counterintelligence Program is now being expanded to include 41 offices. ... For maximum effectiveness of the Counterintelligence Program, and to prevent wasted effort, long-range goals are being set.

1. Prevent the coalition of militant Black Nationalist groups. In unity there is strength; a truism that is no less valid for all its triteness. An effective coalition of Black Nationalist groups might be the first step toward a real "Mau Mau" in America, the beginning of a true black revolution.

2. Prevent the rise of a "messiah" who could unify, and electrify, the militant Black Nationalist movement. Malcolm X might have been such a "messiah;" he is the martyr of the movement today. Martin Luther King, Stokely Carmichael and Elijah Muhammad all aspire to this position. Elijah Muhammad is less of a threat because of his age. King could be a very real contender for this position should he abandon his supposed "obedience" to "white, liberal doctrines" (nonviolence) and embrace Black Nationalism. Carmichael has the necessary charisma to be a real threat in this way.

3. Prevent violence on the part of Black Nationalist groups. This is of primary importance, and is, of course, a goal of our investigative activity; it should also be a goal of the Counterintelligence Program. Through counterintelligence it should be possible to pinpoint potential troublemakers and neutralize them before they exercise their potential for violence.

4. Prevent militant Black Nationalist groups and leaders from gaining respectability, by discrediting them to three separate segments of the community. The goal of discrediting black nationalists must be handled tactically in three ways. You must discredit these groups and individuals to, first, the responsible Negro community. Second, they must be discredited to the white community, both the responsible community and to "liberals" who have vestiges of sympathy for militant black nationalists simply because they are Negroes. Third, these groups must be discredited in the eyes of Negro radicals, the followers of the movement. This last area requires entirely different tactics from the first two. Publicity about violent tendencies and radical statements merely enhances black nationalists black nationalists to the last group; it adds "respectability" in a different way.

5. A final goal should be to prevent the long-range growth of militant Black Nationalist organizations, especially among youth. Specific tactics to prevent these groups from converting young people must be developed. (Sent by Director to Field Offices on March 4, 1968) **G.C. Moore to W.C. Sullivan, Feb. 29, 1968**

Under COINTELPRO the FBI went to extreme lengths by utilizing infiltrators (agents and informants), intimidation, harassment, violence and assassinations. They started a "state of the art" bogus letter writing campaign where they would send threatening letters and false information and then forge the signature of one organizer and send it to another. They even went as far as putting out a racist, violent children's coloring book to deter supporters. Within a year after documents on COINTELPRO were exposed, J. Edgar Hoover announced that the counterinsurgency program was over. But was it really over? Emphatically no!

The Palmer Raids

Before we prove that COINTELPRO still exists or in fact never ended, let's travel back almost four decades prior to 1956, before COINTELPRO in name was birthed. Immediately after World War I, Attorney General Alexander Mitchell Palmer organized the General Intelligence Unit within the Department of Justice and recruited J. Edgar Hoover, a 24-year-old law school graduate who spent the war working in and then leading the Justice Department's Enemy Alien Bureau.

J. Edgar Hoover was the son of, Dickerson Hoover, who was a printer, who had a mental breakdown and spent the last years of his life in an asylum. After the death of his father, Hoover got a position as a messenger boy in the Library of Congress, and in the evenings he studied for his Law Degree at George Washington University.

After graduating in 1917, Hoover's uncle who was a judge helped him find work in the Justice Department. After two years in the department, Palmer appointed Hoover his special assistant. Hoover was given the task of heading a new sector that had been formed to gather evidence on "revolutionary and ultra-revolutionary groups". Over the next couple of years Hoover was responsible for making the arrest and deportation of suspected "communists" in America.

Palmer launched his campaign against radicalism in November 1919 and January 1920 with a series of police actions known as the Palmer Raids. Federal agents backed by local police rounded up large groups of suspected radicals, often based on membership in a political group rather than any action taken. Undercover informants and warrantless wiretaps authorized under the Sedition Act, helped to identify at least 10,000 suspected leftists and radicals arrested.

Hoover, influenced by his work at the Library of Congress, decided to create a massive card index of people with left-wing political views. Over the next few years 450,000 names were indexed and detailed biographical notes were written up on the 60,000 that Hoover considered the most dangerous. Hoover then advised Palmer to have these people rounded up and deported. Due to the lack of evidence, Assistant Secretary of Labor, Louis Freeland Post limited the number of deportations to 556 and dismissed most of the cases.

Hoover was appointed director of the Bureau of Investigation in 1924. The three years that he had spent in the organization had convinced Hoover that the organization needed to improve the quality of its staff. Great care was spent in recruiting and training agents. In 1926, Hoover established a fingerprint file that eventually became the largest in the world.

The power of the bureau was limited. Law enforcement was a state activity, not a federal one. Hoover's agents were not allowed to carry guns, nor did they have the right to arrest suspects. Hoover complained about this situation and in 1935 Congress agreed to establish the Federal Bureau of Investigation (FBI). Agents were now armed and could terrorize citizens under the guise of "acting against crimes of violence".

NOW-INTELPRO

"Take one person that's responsible for unifying the people and assassinate his character and then you assassinate him, then people are confused about his character. They become confused about his character, further confused about his character assassination and even more confused about his actual assassination"- Bilal Sunni-Ali

As stated earlier, one year after COINTELPRO was exposed J. Edgar Hoover announced that the operation had been disbanded. Of course, there are those of us who know better.

As proof that COINTELPRO is alive and well here are a couple examples you may or may not be familiar with:

The Assassination of Tupac Shakur

The government orchestrated infamous "East-West rap beef" between Notorious B.I.G. and Tupac Shakur. Tupac, the son of two former Black Panthers, Afeni Shakur and his stepfather Dr. Mutulu Shakur (currently a political prisoner), was assassinated due to his family background and political beliefs. Tupac grew up surrounded by Panthers who influenced every aspect of his life, so as a multiplatinum recording artist/actor the government knew that it was necessary to neutralize him. Why assassinate an artist? With Tupac's understanding of the oppressive role that the government plays in this society and the impact he had on the youth globally, it was absolutely necessary for them to get rid of him before he began to awaken the masses.

The Notorious B.I.G. on the other hand, an apolitical rapper who was later killed as well, being the most popular rap artist on the East Coast, was simply used as a tool to make the beef look authentic.

It should be noted that shortly after the assassination of Tupac, his cousin Yafu Kadaffi was also assassinated. Kadaffi just so happened to be the son of another prominent movement figure, Sekou Odinga, who is also currently a political prisoner.

The San Francisco 8

In 1971, John Young, a police sergeant was murdered in an Ingleside California station attack. Immediately, several members of the Black Panther Party were arrested and charged with that murder and conspiracy to murder police officers amongst other crimes. In 1973, three members of the Black Panther Party—John Bowman and Ruben Scott, both San Francisco Panthers; and Harold Taylor, who was a Panther from Los Angeles—were arrested in New Orleans. There were 13 Panthers arrested all together. They were separated and they were tortured for days. They were all stripped naked, handcuffed, isolated, repeatedly beaten, and denied sleep and food. They were beaten around the stomach and back. They used slapjacks on their shins and legs, where torturers are trained to beat people so the wounds won't show. They used what is called waterboarding now. Technically what they were using was hot and wet blankets. Also, plastic bags were placed over their heads until the point where they would pass out. They used electrical cattle prods to their private parts and to their anus.

Ed Erdelatz and Frank McCoy were San Francisco homicide detectives and had run-ins with the Panthers long before the Ingleside case. In 1973, they were in New Orleans. Their part was that they never actually touched them. They would come into the room along with the detectives from New York, Los Angeles, and the FBI. They would come in and ask questions and if the questions weren't answered to their satisfaction they would leave the room and the New Orleans Police Department would come in and they would start the torture. Actually the torture started before the questioning began. They arrested them, took them in, stripped them, isolated them and just started beating them. They just enjoyed torture. They would do a job on them and then leave and tell them 'we'll be back.' Then the detectives would come in and start asking questions.

First the Brothers would try and tell the detectives that they were being tortured and then the detectives would get up and walk out of the room and the New Orleans police would come in. This went on for days. They would keep them up at night, not allow them to sleep. Wake them up every hour or so. Throw water-soaked blankets on them, scalding hot water so they couldn't breathe. This is the treatment that they had to endure for days. When the case was taken to court in 1975, the three people charged, John Bowman, Ruben Scott, and Harold Taylor all stated that they were tortured and forced to confess. Because of that and the fact that they were questioned without any attorney being present in New Orleans, the court threw the so-called "admission of guilt" and the case out.

In 2003, thirty years after the tortures, Ed Erdelatz and Frank McCoy were brought out of retirement and deputized by Homeland Security and they went knocking on the brother's doors during a grand jury investigation asking, 'Do you remember me?' and giving them subpoenas to appear before a grand jury. Imagine the same goons that were responsible for your torture showing up at your doorstep, three decades later. "In 1971, two brothers and I were set up by the FBI. We didn't learn about COINTELPRO until years later. In 1973 I was arrested in New Orleans and was beaten and tortured for several days. In 2003 the detectives that were responsible for my torture came to my house to try and question me. I have not been the same since" (Harold Taylor).

In 2005, the accused men all refused to testify before the grand jury. Five of the men were held in contempt of court:

Hank Jones, Ray Boudreaux, Harold Taylor, Richard Brown and John Bowman (now deceased).

In January of 2007, they re-arrested eight of the men for the same crime and the same charges. These men became know as the San Francisco 8. They are Francisco Torres, Herman Bell, Ray Boudreaux, Richard Brown, Hank Jones, Jalil Muntaqim, Richard O'Neal, and Harold Taylor. As of this writing charges have been dropped against Richard Brown, Harold Taylor, Ray Boudreaux, Richard O'Neal and Hank Jones. Herman Bell and Jalil Muntaqim, who have been in prison in New York for almost 40 years on similar COINTELPRO charges were sentenced to probation and time served, after Herman agreed to plead to voluntary manslaughter and Jalil to conspiracy to voluntary manslaughter. The remaining SF8 member, Francisco Torres is still facing charges and in between court dates.

These are just a couple of the countless examples of how COINTELPRO continues to devastate the lives of our people on all levels, whether its outright murder, state sponsored kidnappings or character assassination the fact remains that there is a continuous war being waged on the people. With that in mind a light weight historical glance will prove that any nation that wanted to maintain an oppressive strong hold over a people had to have some form of counter intelligence program to prevent an uprising or coup to overthrow their regime. We are also clear that informants, snitches and agent provocateurs are the eyes, ears and puppets of the United States government and other nations whose chief means of survival is through the exploitation and oppression of the masses. Knowing the serious nature of working on behalf of the people, we expect there to be informants and infiltrators within the ranks.That's what comes with warfare. As Kwame Ture would say, "If I'm hunting my enemy and my enemy ain't hunting me, then what am I doing wrong?" That's why it is best to keep a small, efficient team and you get to know each others' strengths and weaknesses, and above all stay clean and stay public. My Grandmother told me a long time ago, "Don't tell everybody everything or they will know as much as you".

On Sept. 12, 2010 *The Commercial Appeal,* a Memphis newspaper reported that famed photographer Ernest Withers was as an FBI informant and spied on Dr. Martin Luther King and the civil rights movement. According to the newspaper, Mr. Withers whose photography ranged from the murder of 14-year-old Emmett Till in 1955, to the 1968 assassination of Dr. Martin Luther King, Jr., shadowed King the day before his murder, snapping photos and telling agents about a meeting the civil rights leader had with suspected black militants. According to the Memphis article Civil Rights Activist Andrew Young stated that he wasn't bothered that Withers secretly worked as an informant while snapping civil rights history. The paper went on to quote him as saying, "I always liked him because he was a good photographer-I don't think Dr. King would have minded him making a little money on the side."

During an interview with *The Final Call* newspaper for a story entitled, "*Government infiltration threatens rights and freedom, warn analysts*", I was asked by the interviewer, Eric Ture Muhammad what I thought about Mr. Young's statement, I responded by saying, "With all due respect to Andy Young, I think that is one of the most absurd statements that an educated man can make in these days and times. Saying that he thinks that Dr. King wouldn't have minded this man making money snitching on his people is almost equivalent to saying he wouldn't have minded a prostitute making a little money selling her body." Noted activist/comedian Dick Gregory who was also asked the same question during the interview answered by saying, "Can you imagine a Jew in Nazi Germany finding out that a Jew was working with Hitler for the Nazis and then another Jew saying we wouldn't have minded him making a little money on the side?" Maybe Andrew Young didn't look at it that way. It is NEVER acceptable to turn for the enemy. Playing with your enemy is like playing with fire-someone or something will eventually get burned.

Cyber Snitches, Internet Informants and Tele-terrorist

Unfortunately, counterinsurgency is still in full effect; you have to be critical & analytical. You can't believe everything you read or hear. In the 60's, part of Cointelpro was the letter writing campaign, now-a-days it's the Internet. The Internet is a gift and a curse, it's a way to get information out, but it's also the devil's playground. Just because you log onto a so-called "Revolutionary" website, doesn't mean that it's not government sponsored and setup to purposely mislead and misinform the people. It doesn't matter what Freedom Fighter's name is being used. You have one or two people with 20 websites set up in the name of legitimate forces with the sole purpose of confusing the masses.

In 2006, it was discovered that the US Military was actually paying bloggers to create bogus sites to discredit groups and individuals. There was a study, written for U.S. Special Operations Command, which suggested, "clandestinely recruiting or hiring prominent bloggers." This 2006 report for the Joint Special Operations University, "Blogs and Military Information Strategy," discussed co-opting bloggers, or even putting them on the payroll. It suggested "Hiring a block of bloggers to verbally attack a specific person or promote a specific message may be worth considering".

Coincidentally, 2006 was the same year that an Atlanta based web group known as "The Talking Drum Collective" began an Internet smear campaign against members of our organization, The FTP Movement and myself. Since that campaign began the group has made an effort to discredit our organization by slandering us on well over a 150 blogs, social forums and websites.

The Talking Drum Collective owned and operated by Johnnie D. Walker aka Jacuma Kambui and his partners Darnell Crawford along with Darnell's girlfriend, Alexis Lucas are the creators of www.thetalkingdrum.com, www.Assatashakur.org, and about two dozen other sites. On May 10, 2010, after 4 years of the Talking Drum Collective's ongoing internet slander campaign against us and erecting numerous false websites in our name, it was brought to our attention by supporters of our organization, that there had been another fraudulent site set up in our name that featured our logo and a phony version of one of the programs we established with links to a PayPal account in which they were collecting financial contributions from our supporters.

It should be noted that after doing a People's Investigation it was discovered that at least one member of The Talking Drum Collective- Darnell Crawford, worked as an Information Specialist for the Tank and Armament division of the U.S. Army, in Michigan.

When asked why I think these people have spent so much time attacking us, my response is that it's bigger than us and it's bigger than them. It's an attack on youth movements and any potential uprisings. They just happen to be pawns in the game-a game in which they will not be victorious.

So it was in the 60's as it is today. During the 60's we know that there were several different military and police agencies whose purpose was to douse the flames of resistance. Different tactics from fake letter writing campaigns, framings, false imprisonment and murder. Front and center was the FBI contriving all types of chaos via COINTELPRO. During this era, participants in the struggle had no idea that they were a part of a calculated hit orchestrated by the U S government. What amazes me is that over a decade into the 21st century, the same tactics are being used and some of the same participants who survived the 60's COINTELPRO attacks still don't recognize it when they see it, as if it is some type of Post Traumatic Syndrome. All of the aforementioned tactics are still being utilized, except with technology the letter writing campaign has advanced to Internet assaults.

Still not convinced that the FBI would utilize bloggers as a modern day tool for COINTELPRO tactics? In 2008, a group of unknown hackers broke into an e-mail account belonging to radio shock jock/ blogger Hal Turner. During the hacking it was discovered and exposed that Turner was a paid FBI informant and agent provocateur. Hal Turner admitted that he had been hired by the FBI in 2002 to infiltrate supremacist organizations such as the Patriot Movement. "His job was basically to publish information which would cause other parties to act in a manner which would lead to their arrest," Michael Orozco, Hal Turner's Attorney. According to Orozco, "Mr. Turner was trained by the FBI on how to be deliberately provocative" and "he worked for the FBI from 2002 to 2007 as an 'agent provocateur' and was taught by the agency what he could say that wouldn't be crossing the line." During his five-year

138

stint as an FBI patsy Turner was paid $100,000 and he shared his racist rants on everything from "shooting Mexicans as they crossed the border" to "lynching Congresswoman Cynthia McKinney". In 2006, he stated that, "Cynthia McKinney is a violent, black, racist, bitch whose official re-election campaign web site calls white people 'crackers'. As such, on this Wednesday evening's show I will ask the question 'Given the prevalence of black crime in America, would it serve the public good to LYNCH Congresswoman McKinney within the next few weeks, while she's on the campaign trail, so as to send an unmistakable message to other blacks: white people are tired of your bullshit, behave or die."

At the time he made those remarks the Congresswoman was still in office and Turner received no reprimand. He got away scot-free and continued with business as usual. In June of 2009, after the FBI found no more use of him, Turner made threats against Connecticut legislators and wrote that three federal judges in Illinois deserved to die.

Mr. Turner urged his readers to 'take up arms' against Connecticut lawmakers and suggested government officials should 'obey the Constitution or die,' because he was angry over legislation — later withdrawn — that would have given lay members of Roman Catholic churches more control over their parish's finances.

In the same month, Turner posted on the Internet that the Illinois federal appeals judges 'deserve to be killed' because they issued a ruling that upheld ordinances in Chicago and suburban Oak Park banning handguns. He included the judge's photos, addresses, telephone numbers and a complete map along with the room numbers of their chambers at the courthouse.

In a show of gratitude for his years of service, the FBI, the same agency that he worked for arrested him in his home in New Jersey.

On August 13th 2010, Turner was sentenced to 10 years in prison and he has to pay a $250,000 fine. The price of a rat!

For clarity, I mentioned the case of Hal Turner as evidence that the feds haven't ended their lies and trickery, if anything they have enhanced and perfected them. I by no means feel anything in regards to Hal Turner; in fact I feel he got what he deserved. No matter what euphemism is used, whether it's the Patriot Act, the war on terror, the war on drugs or what have you at the end of the day its still the same ol' shit. There have been many cases of informants and agent provocateurs playing roles in not only organizations, but also events and criminal cases.

So you have to be careful, if you don't see the people you deal with online in the community sometimes you have to treat them like entertainment. Also, the folks that you roll with, you should re-evaluate your relationships and remember under what circumstances you met, who introduced you and what kind of credentials they have. You should be able to run a reference check on any new or existing folks. Sometimes as organizers people let there guards down out of desperation. Never get caught up in the numbers, the more members you have the less control you have of a situation. Watch out for attention cravers, addicts, overly emotional troops, folks with psychological issues or those who have legal issues over their heads-those are the best qualified infiltrators and provocateurs. Stay on point and in the words of Muhammad Ahmed (Formerly Max Stanford of RAM), "conspicuous consumption and foolish wasting of time must come to a prompt and immediate end. Slaves have no time to party".

Bang On Da System

I simmer in the pain of death.
But, I ain't dead yet.
Capitalistic Oppression
Globally Afrikans live in recession.
From cradle to grave,
Niggas walking around with Obama blinders on
Like all is good, 'n we were never slaves.
Master still fucking us masked in black face.
My enemy's enemy is an ally
New World Order elitists really don't give a fuck about
race.
However, There are still some subordinate fascist pale face
Who thinks that's the case.
'N if any cracker should step
I vow to wipe them out
As smoothly as I take a breath.
You can kill a revolutionary
Yet, The essence of revolution transcends death.
So neither fear nor fret,
For revolution is my reparations 'n my salvation.
So I won't rest until the last mouth is fed
'N all Afrikans are free.
Uhuru Sasa
F.T.P.

Imhotep Kushan

The People's Congresswoman Cynthia McKinney on COINTELPRO, Tupac Shakur and The Black Panther Party

(Excerpt from a June 2006 Interview)

Kalonji: What is the Martin Luther King Jr. Records Act and how does it relate to rapper Tupac Shakur?

C. McKinney: I have been interested in COINTELPRO - the counterintelligence program for a long time. My interest originally arose because I was trying to figure out why my young Black Son didn't have proud Black adult male role models, or that they were limited in number. Yet the African American Men, who were prominently portrayed by the mainstream media, were not exactly what I would call positive role models for my son. Then my search for an answer took me to the volumes around COINTELPRO. Of course the definitive work is that done by Ward Churchill, which is a compilation and dissection of the COINTELPRO papers. Once I got into the mindset of U.S. Government employees, who would basically disrupt marriages, orchestrate and even incite murder, I began to ask the question, "Well what happened in the murder of Dr. King"? At that point I hooked up with a gentleman who is the executive director, on a volunteer basis, of an organization called The Committee on Political Assassinations (COPA), his name is John Judge. COPA has assigned to itself the herculean task of going through the millions of pages of documents relating to the murder of JFK. So I began to ask, "Do you have any papers relating to the murder of MLK"? So they began to broaden their search and there was one document in particular, that's not included in the book, The COINTELPRO Papers. It's a May 11, 1965 document that says, "Somewhere at the top there must be a Negro who is clean, who can step into the

142

vacuum once Dr. King is either exposed or assassinated". That sentence stuck out in my mind for many reasons, because it says a lot. First of all, it says that they were looking for what they considered to be "Clean Negroes" and that means they were looking for acceptable Black People to assume the mantle of leadership of the African American Community. In the COINTELPRO papers they said they would never allow another Martin Luther King to rise. But here we have a document, here fore unknown, that's talking about Dr. King's assassination. Also, it intimates a policy of regime change on Black America. There in that one sentence, in that one document, is a description of the affliction that continues to this day to affect the Black Community in America. Then I decided that I would join with John Judge, who is now on the congressional staff and we work on these issues full time. It was before he joined the staff that we came up with the idea of drafting the Bill. Then after he joined the staff we drafted the Bill. We contacted various African American organizations, such as The National Bar Association, The Association of Black Librarians, and The Black Political Scientists. People who deal with political documents and documents in terms of archiving them. We began to contact them and include them as resources as we began to draft the Bill. We used the Martin Luther King Records Act as a template for the Tupac Shakur Records Act. Just as they have a myth that is not true about the murder of Dr. King, we also do not have the truth about the murder of Tupac Shakur. It will be my efforts for, as many days as I remain in the United States Congress - I want to find the truth and provide the truth to the American people, who need to know the truth. The things that were done in the COINTELPRO era against Americans of conscience were illegal then. But now we have an administration that chooses to either change the law, as in the Patriot Act, which is really Un-Patriotic, or to ignore the law as in the secret wire tapping of American citizens. More than ever, with the revelations of police surveillance of Hip Hop cultural icons, we need to know exactly what this government is capable of, so that we can adequately protect ourselves.

Kalonji: Why is it important to investigate the murder of Tupac Shakur?

C. McKinney: I think knowing the truth, that Tupac was murdered. You notice I don't say, "died" with Tupac and I don't say, "died" with Dr. King, because they were both murdered. We need to understand the language we use is very powerful in the way we think about things. These people were murdered, I believe, because they had vision. They had the power of persuasion over Black People and White People. They had conscience. If you look at what J. Edgar Hoover wrote in the first document that opens Ward Churchill's COINTELPRO Papers book, what J. Edgar Hoover wrote was in October of 1919 about Marcus Garvey. He said, "He excites the Negroes". Now, let's look at the fate of Black People who have "excited the Negroes" in America. It's been a whole lot of bloodshed, a whole lot of murder. If I go back and I look at what happened before, during the COINTELPRO days, if I understand the motivation from the Marcus Garvey experience, then I will have a basis on which to judge what's happening today. Remember, it's closer to you because you're a whole lot younger than I am. I was a distant observer, not really fully appreciative earlier on, or else I would have intervened to try to stop it. The East Coast-West Coast conundrum that overtook the Hip Hop Movement was exactly the same phenomenon that accelerated the dissipation of The Black Panther Party. From the COINTELPRO papers, we know that the FBI incited that. So if they would do it to The Black

Panther Party, why wouldn't they do it to young, culturally rich, politically potent, African American Men? Then we know that point # 5, on the founding COINTELPRO document, written March 1968, was directed at preventing young Blacks from adhering to a Black Nationalist ideology. They wrote that down. Tupac was steeped in Black Nationalism, with the wonderful philosophical militantism of his mother, and the men around him. So Tupac understood that the plight of African Americans in this country, was not due to African American misbehavior, but it was due to structural inequities that were built into the American system, and that the system itself would have to be attacked.

Kalonji: Do you think it may be possible, that the assassination of Tupac could have been a Political hit?

C. McKinney: I could tell you that I have seen reports that there's one particular organization that was involved in death threats against Tupac and shaking him down for money. That same organization was linked in the COINTELPRO papers, to the demise of The Black Panther Party. So those are two dots, upon further study that might be connected.

Kalonji: Do you feel that COINTELPRO still exists today in 2006?

C. McKinney: Absolutely. The White House has an enemies list and they keep documents on more than 10,000 names, utilizing FBI records. This Bush Administration has an active enemies list. We don't know what happens to those people. But, I can tell you strange things happen to my computer and my telephone (laughs)....

Kalonji: Now, why would they bother you (laughs)? We

discussed COINTELPRO; there was a case right here in Atlanta involving Imam Jamil Al-Amin (formerly H. Rap Brown), where he was accused of killing a deputy sheriff and wounding another. Based on evidence, there was nothing linking him to the scene of the crime, could that possibly be a COINTELPRO move?

C. McKinney: I have since learned that former members of The Black Panther Party and their children have all been targeted in various different ways. I have also learned that even the Black Activists who are now prisoners of conscience, that they have been singled out for "special treatment", that is not good. It is clear that not only a new form of COINTELPRO exists, with a much broader administration, but also they haven't left alone the activists from the COINTELPRO days. Not only the Black Activists but, the Native Americans Activists such as Leonard Peltier as well. Then what they did to the Brothers in Puerto Rico and all the people of color who were activists during the COINTELPRO days who continue to be targeted as well.

Kalonji: It was alleged, that you were one of the members of Congress who signed to have Assata Shakur extradited back to the U.S., can you speak on that?

C. McKinney: During the first time I was in Congress, the republicans pushed a resolution that came to the floor of the house about a woman, and to be honest with you, I can't remember her other name, and that was the name on the resolution. I remember many of the Congress members were asking, "what is this?" we didn't know what it was. I was with Maxine at the time of the vote and we didn't know who this person was, now of course, we know it was Assata Shakur. I don't think any such legislation has been revisited by Congress. I know in the Black Community, the young people stood up, and I would hope that some of the white members of Congress were approached as well. Maybe that's the reason why the Bill hasn't come up again.

Kalonji: A little over a year ago, the FBI issued a One Million Dollar Bounty on the head of Assata Shakur, why are they still hunting her?

C. McKinney: This is consistent with what I have learned about the U.S. Government continuing to target activist from the COINTELPRO days. Crimes committed against people of color in this country.

Kalonji: In 2000 you organized a forum in D.C. on Political Prisoners, will there be a follow up?

C. McKinney: That was the first of our COINTELPRO hearings and then we did the second one on Dr. Martin Luther King Jr., then I got kicked out of Congress for 2 years. Last year we continued the COINTELPRO theme with what we called "Countering Culture: The Attack on our Culture Icons". We focused on Bob Marley, Tupac, Paul Robeson and Jimi Hendrix. We are continuing to shed the light on this issue, which never gets coverage from the mainstream media. This is life and death for our Community because in my opinion, this is a form of genocide. Genocide is the elimination in whole or part of a people. If you deny people the right to select their own leaders, then they cannot adequately address the political system with their grievances. They are sending us to jail and we don't know what they are doing to our young men and women in these prisons. With the DNA swabs, and building the DNA Banks, that's a whole other issue of technology against our people that we need to be dealing with that we're not. Our people are experiencing death prematurely because of lack of access to healthcare. Then our people are not being educated due to the lack of access to adequate education. All these are results of not having people who are placing demands on the political system. Those demands are not being placed on the political system because those people who are selected Black Leaders are often not the choice of Black People.

A Victim of American Politics: The Case of Troy Anthony Davis

Excerpt from interview with Martina Correia (July 2007)

The first time I heard of Troy Anthony Davis was Monday July 10th 2007, one week before his first scheduled July 17th execution date. I had gotten a call from Dhoruba Bin Wahad (who was in New Jersey at the time) saying that we had to do something to stop the state from killing this Brother. I told him that I knew nothing about the case. The strange thing about it was that there was absolutely no news coverage. No one I talked to knew anything about it so clearly the State of Georgia had every intention of killing him without any noise from the Black community. Dhoruba reached out to a mutual comrade, Kazi Toure, who happened to know a Sister who was organizing around the case in Savannah and he passed Dhoruba her number and he forwarded the number to me. I called the Sister, Aleeta Toure and asked her to fill me in on the case. She broke it down and ended it by telling me "they will be killing an innocent man next week". I asked her what was going on in Savannah that week and if there were any rallies, protests, marches or anything of that nature and she told me that nothing was happening. I expressed to her that we needed to do something and that if she could get a venue that I would help her organize a program in Savannah for that weekend. The next day she informed me that she had gotten a catholic church to allow a rally in there building. Over the next few days we organized the event, which took, place that Saturday (July 14th). Comrade Taj Anwar and myself drove to Savannah to take part in what turned out to be a successful event with a great turnout. On that Monday July 16th, 24 hours before the scheduled execution, Troy received a 90-day stay of execution. And that's when the name Troy Davis was thrust into the international headlines.

The case of Troy Anthony Davis has all the ingredients of a bad movie. Troy Davis a caring well-mannered young Black Man was raised by two loving parents in a small section of Savannah, Georgia. His mother was a former Civil Rights worker and his father a Savannah Police Officer, for a police department that during the 1970's, didn't allow black officers to arrest whites. Despite being morally sound, and as some people that knew him describe him, "a man of excellent character"; in 1989, Troy was accused and convicted of the murder of Savannah police officer Mark Macphail. Throughout the trial Troy maintained his innocence, however there were 9 witnesses who each fingered Troy as the assailant. The outcome, Troy Anthony Davis was convicted as a cop killer and sentenced to die by execution in the State of Georgia.

Case Closed? Not quite. As time went on the witnesses who testified against Troy began to one by one, admit that they were coerced and if not forced to testify against Troy by Savannah police. Summing it up plainly, they were directed and if not willing then threatened to lie. Seven out of nine witnesses recanted their stories, the eighth witness said he was certain the shooter was left-handed (Troy is right-handed) and the 9th is the suspect. One witness, who was16 years old at the time, stated that the police told him that if he didn't testify he would go to jail as an accessory. Another female was on parole and threatened with jail time and another was an illiterate man forced to sign a confession he couldn't even read. With 88% of the witnesses recanting their testimonies, *Free Troy Petitions*, and the support of numerous anti-death penalty/grass root organizations; the state was now forced to give Troy a 90-day stay of execution.

Troy 's case has garnered support from notables such as Bishop Desmond Tutu, Harry Belafonte, former FBI William Sullivan (who is pro-death penalty) and even the Pope. But despite such support and even the lack of evidence that still remains today from the Savannah Police Department, Governor Sonny Purdue won't budge and Officer Macphail's widow still wants to see Troy Anthony Davis executed.

We went to Troy Davis' old neighborhood to talk to some of the older folks in the community and there Troy received nothing but praise. We even went to the home of one of the witnesses who had testified and he talked about how he was pressured into falsely accusing Troy. Soon it became obvious that the man the media has depicted as a monster not only comes from a strong, committed and loving family but that there is something gravely disturbing about this case. So what's really going on? And can we find out before a man who has been wrongfully sentenced to death is executed because of the malfeasance and negligence of state officials and the media?

The following is an up close and personal interview with Martina Correia, sister of Troy Davis:

Kalonji: Who is Troy Davis and how did this case come about?

Martina: Troy Davis is a 38-year-old African American male who has been on death row for 16 years. In 1989 he was accused of killing an off duty police officer in a Burger King parking lot in Savannah, Ga. What took place was Troy and some friends were playing pool and a homeless man was going into a convenience store to buy some beer and one of the other gentlemen that was playing pool began harassing the homeless man over a can of beer and followed him up the street. After arguing with him, he began pistol-whipping him (the homeless man) and Troy and another man went up to him to try to intervene. The man who was pistol whipping the homeless man, his name is Sylvester Coles, then turned the gun on Troy and the other young man and said, " You don't know me nigga, I'll shoot you". So they turned off and they left. As they were leaving someone was yelling for help and an off duty police officer came out and he was shot. He was shot in the arm then the bullet ricocheted and then he was shot in the face. Nobody knew what took place and all the witnesses identified the shooter as the man in the parking lot because that's who had the weapon. Probably about 10-12 hours later, Sylvester had changed his clothes, threw away his gun, went to the police department with his lawyer, asked for immunity and pointed the finger at Troy Davis. The police went to my mother's house, got a picture of Troy and the next day they put his picture in the paper saying they were looking for a cop killer. They didn't have any physical evidence, no weapons, and no gunpowder residue, nothing against Troy. They only had 9 eyewitnesses. And since the trial, when Troy was put on death row our family was not allowed to go into the courtroom and the only time we were allowed to go into the courtroom was to beg for Troy's life. Since Troy 's death sentence 7 of the 9 witnesses have recanted their statements and said the police threatened them, coerced them, challenged them and threatened them with jail time. Now the case against Troy is two witnesses, really one considering one is the actual shooter. The other witness said that all he knew is the person was left- handed and Troy is right- handed. Troy was scheduled to be executed on the 17th of July and if we don't get him a new trial or get someone to intervene on the parole board for clemency then Troy will be executed before October 2007.

Kalonji: So 7 of the 9 eyewitnesses recanted their statements, another said the shooter was left-handed and the 9th is the suspect, is that right?

Martina: That's correct. And there is an additional 2 to 3 dozen witnesses that have come forward and testified by signed affidavit that Sylvester Coles has been bragging throughout the community that he is the shooter and there were actually two witnesses on the scene that testified that he was the shooter, but the police tried to discredit them. So there are people who name him as the shooter as well as witnesses who have recanted. They really don't have a case against Troy except for Sylvester Coles, who owned the same caliber weapon that the police officer was shot with and that is a .38 caliber weapon, which he never produced.

Kalonji: When did these witnesses recant their statements and why haven't the courts accepted these statements?

Martina: One witness recanted at trial, another shortly after trial so they were trying to say (the state) that the witnesses were being intimidated by Troy Davis across the courtroom. The other witnesses started coming forth 3-4 years after Troy was on death row because they didn't think that Troy would be put on death row for their statements. So what happened was the 1996 anti-terrorism law, signed into law by Bill Clinton, states that you can only introduce new evidence for up to 2 years after your conviction. Well Troy didn't have a lawyer after his conviction. The resource center that was trying to help him is a pro bono law firm, but when you have 1 lawyer handling 80 cases etc.... So what happened was the only time they would work on your death penalty case is when they had to file something and sometimes that was 1 or 2 weeks before it was due. Therefore when the witnesses started coming forth and the lawyers were not in place to investigate, they had passed the 2 years after the conviction. So what Troy has been fighting has not been an actual innocence case, he has been fighting to get his information heard, because of a federal law technicality that says you don't have to look at actual innocence if there is a procedural error.

Kalonji: On Monday July 16th, 24 hours before the scheduled execution, Troy received a 90-day stay of execution. How did that come about and what does that mean?

Martina: The defense put up their case before the parole board and the state put up their case before the parole board. The state had the victim's family and the defense had the defendant's family. We were in the parole hearing for 5 hours and it was very extensive. There were witnesses there who were questioned by the parole board members. Family members spoke and friends spoke on behalf of Troy and we had to show the there was reasonable doubt and that they should not kill this person if there is reasonable doubt. What happened was since the courts have refused to do their job, the parole board is acting like a court- type system. But all they can do is to commute Troy 's sentence, they can't free Troy and Troy should be pardoned and totally exonerated. Then the prosecutors got to plead their case to tell them not to give Troy clemency, but because there were so many questions and so many concerns and I think the parole board could see the pressure coming from around the world about this concern for innocence, that they gave Troy an up to 90 day stay. Which means that they could revoke that stay at any time and Troy could still be given another execution date. So we really have to work very hard to keep this stay in place and to push for the Georgia Supreme Court to give Troy an evidentiary hearing or for the parole board to give him clemency and the only thing they could do is commute his sentence to life or to life without parole.

Kalonji: Troy has been on death row over 16 years, why haven't we heard about this case?

Martina: First of all, Troy is accused of killing a white police officer in the South. No one wants to cover that story in the news. Second of all, I'm Troy's sister and I've been telling this story for 16-17 years and people would feel I'm biased and maybe not telling the whole truth, even when we give them the information and thirdly, this is the South and when you're dealing with a Black on White crime, even the Black people in the community won't stand up to readily support you. I had to go outside of the country to tell Troy 's story to bring it within the country. Amnesty International came forward with a 35-page report and that's when things started unraveling for Troy and people started seeing what was going on. But by that time the prosecutor started really pushing for an execution because they saw Troy 's case was building momentum. We have been going to organizations for years and we've gotten the same response, "this is a terrible thing, and we wish you luck". So I have been pushing, pushing, pushing to get the story out and now that it's getting out we just have to keep going.

Kalonji: Why do you think the State would like to see Troy Anthony Davis executed?

Martina: Because they don't want to admit the police prose curial misconduct. They don't want people to say that they are killing an innocent person. They want Troy to go and die quietly, so that they can appease the people in the White community. They didn't care what Troy said in the courtroom. He could have said anything in the courtroom, someone else could have confessed to the crime in the courtroom. They had vilified and hated Troy in the White community and some people in the Black community for 2 years before trial, so it didn't matter what he had to say. They had no physical evidence. He was tried in the media and the newspaper and so they just wanted a Black man for this crime, they knew that someone Black had shot this police officer and they didn't care who they got.

Kalonji: What can the people on the grassroots level do to support Troy at this stage in the game?

Martina: Get Troy 's story told in all the Black newspapers, college papers, radio and other forms of media. They could go to www.troyanthonydavis.org and sign an online letter, send it to the parole board. Even if they have signed an older letter for Troy, there is an updated letter on his site. We need a 100,000 letters or more signed and sent to the parole board. We need letters sent to every major newspaper in the country. Let them know we need to free Troy Davis and we will not stand for innocent people being executed. And we will not stand for Black men being made examples of any longer in the South.

** Since this interview, Troy has had two more stays of execution and the Supreme Court still refuses to hear his case. Our organization has traveled to Savannah on several occasions and witnessed the blatant aged racism first hand. On one occasion, while petitioning an old white man said to our Comrade Eboni Joy," I hope they fry the Nigger". Another said to me, "we freed you 'Niggras' from slavery, what else do you want". This didn't take place in the sixties this was 2011- with a Black President in office. That's just an idea of the mind state of the geographical location that we are seeking justice from. It is crucial for anyone with a conscience to support Troy Anthony Davis. If the state has their way Troy will die by lethal injection. We need any and everyone that reads this to spread the information, write letters to the parole board, make phone calls, send emails, Facebook, Twitter etc. We urge you for the sake of humanity to fight not only on the behalf of Troy Davis but for oppressed and wrongfully accused people worldwide.
For more information and updates please go to: www.Troyanthonydavis.org

Free Troy Davis and all political prisoners and victims of American politics! Rest in Uhuru to Troy's mother, Missionary Virginia Davis, a powerful, faithful woman who made her transition on April 12, 2011. It was an honor being in your midst and we will continue the fight until Troy walks from behind enemy lines a free man.

BEHIND ENEMY LINES

Behind Enemy Lines is a campaign developed to fight for the liberation of Political Prisoners and Falsely accused victims incarcerated by a cruel and injustice "legal" system.

WHAT IS A POLITICAL PRISONER?

A Political Prisoner is someone who was targeted and imprisoned because of his or her political actions, affiliations and/or beliefs. A political prisoner is also a person who takes up and maintains political struggle even when and especially while he or she is in prison, and is often segregated from the regular prison population to keep him/her from influencing and transforming others into recruits for the movement. He is a threat to prison security and management because he stands in direct and perpetual opposition to the whole complex of reasons and ideas that support the prison and its legitimacy. The reasons for denying this kind of prisoner any release back into the prison population or the civilian population are political and have little or nothing to do with the "original offense".

WHY SHOULD THEY BE SUPPORTED?

They should be supported because many of these individuals were committed to confronting the oppression and exploitation in their communities that made their lives and the lives of their neighbors/community intolerable. They were examples of the best of our community and those who follow in their footsteps, knowingly or unknowingly, are likely to be recipients of the same assaults. That means that today's activist (i.e. you and me) may be tomorrow's political prisoner. Anyone who sticks his or her neck out to challenge the system (the

157

government, corporations, etc.) may become a target. Therefore, we need to have a community mindset that we will protect those that protect us.

Write a political prisoner today!
For an updated list of political prisoners email defendingthepoor@yahoo.com

AMERIKKKA THE BEAUTIFUL

Government experiments on military personnel and
civilians without their knowledge or consent.

Bills signed by the governor, surgeon general and
the U.S. President.

War declared via Bio chemical germ warfare on
men, women and children on the African continent.

50 million infected with A.I.D.S.,
30 million Ebola virus.

Center for disease Control and World Health Organization
reach their accomplishment, while frontin' like they got
good intent.

Giving out tainted blood and pinholes in the love gloves,
like it was love.

Why?
Just because cuz'.

And you could tell from the tracks and dope needles
hangin' from my uncle's arms.
I said you could tell from the tracks and dope needles
hangin' from my uncle's arms-hangin' from his goddamn
arms.

Meanwhile, you mutha fuckas talking about
Gunning down Bin Laden and lynching Saddam. My uncle
wakes up in a cardboard box, conversing with himself-
Cold sweating napalm from bombs and Agent Orange from
Vietnam.

Agent orange from Vietnam.
"Soldier tested Government approved".

Transformed my uncle from a warrior.
To a bum in a box who had his legs removed.

And kids poked fun. Adults stared and didn't care.
"Yo, you know that dope head with no legs, they found that
mutha fucka froze to death slumped over in his wheel
chair"!

At a minimal the government's corrupt and criminal.
A.I.D.S. is man made, it didn't come from no green
monkey nor needle-sharing junky.

It was created in 69', Fort Dietrick, Maryland-
By Robert McMann, a Department of Defense/CIA flunky.

Backed by Congress $10 Million is what they spent, it's
documented.
Plus, Attorney Boyd Graves had Exhibit A evidence.

That's why I burn the Amerikkkan flag and yell,
"Fuck the President"!

And you don't have to fly oversees to find a terrorist
system to make ya blood boil,
In 1932 Tuskegee Syphilis Experiment was launched on
200 Black men right here on Amerikkkan soil... Yet still
Amerikkkans are spoiled.

It's time to unfoil these lies and loaded dice.
The devil's Bush, Blair, Clinton, Obama, Powell and
Condoleezza Rice.
And Fuck Rumsfeld, Ashcroft and Tom Ridge.

Where the hell was Homeland Security when they kidnapped and murdered those Atlanta kids, and cut off the foreskins of their penises for melanin to make melatonin.

Now for tampering on holy ground, spirits will rise like the omen.
No more murdering Afrikans, scalping natives,
small pox laced blankets for trinkets.
As we escape the matrix, the government is a fraud.

"Amerikkka, Amerikkka," what the fuck you thinking?
The U.S. is the titanic and the ship is slowly sinking!

REVOLUTIONARY GLOSSARY:

Absolute Equalitarianism: The narrow and fixed view that "all things are created equal" and that every situation, person or policy should be approached and dealt with in uniform manner regardless of the actual circumstances, conditions and needs.

Actor-vist: A person who assumes the role of an activist under false pretense. The individual pretends to work on behalf of the people, when in reality they work for selfish gains i.e. to feed their own ego. An opportunist.

Agent Provocateur: A person who joins a group by pretending to be sympathetic towards the aims of the group and begins to encourage its members to commit illegal acts in which they may cause them to be jailed.

Anarchism: The philosophy of total freedom without any government structure or state. It negates the necessity of the dictatorship of the proletariat to re-educate and organize the masses and protect the gains of the revolution as a transitory stage in the development towards true communism where the state will wither away.

Black Collaborator: Those few Blacks brought into the capitalist system at all levels who feel they have enough at stake in the system to cooperate in pacification programs against their people.

Bourgeoisie: the capitalist class who own most of society's wealth and means of production.

Cadre: Framework; a nucleus of trained, experienced activists in an organization capable of assuming leadership and/or training and educating, others to perform functional roles.

Capitalism: A system of economic exploitation based upon the myth of free enterprise and private ownership of the means of production and profit.

Class Society: A tier system where the people are separated into different categories based upon their financial relationships to the means of production.

Cliqueism: The formation of exclusive groups based upon emotional or opportunistic alliances which negates overall organizational unity.

Collective: A cooperative unit or organization that that utilizes its strength in unity to struggle for common goals and objectives.

Colonialism: Foreign domination of a country or people where the economic, political and military structure is controlled and run by occupying forces.

Comic Books: Literature (including books and dvd's) that distract potential organizers from core issues that affect the community. The authors usually conveniently moonlight as activists when it serves to benefit them either through popularity or economically.

Communism: Social system based on collective ownership of the means of production, the absence of any state apparatus or government control.

Comrade: A soldier or companion who shares one's activities or is a fellow member of an organization. A comrade is not necessarily a friend but one who understands the necessity to work together to accomplish similar or the same goals.

Constructive Criticism: The positive correcting and pointing out of mistaken ideas and incorrect practices and the offering of concrete practical solutions that build instead of tearing down.

Contradiction: A combination of statements, ideas, or features of a situation that are opposed to one another.

Coup: An overthrow.

Coup d'état: The successful overthrow of existing authority in one audacious stroke, usually by a section of the armed forces or a people's army.

Coup de grace: A deathblow or shot administered to end the suffering of one mortally wounded. A decisive finishing blow or event.

Counter Revolution: Someone or something that goes against revolutionary principles and practices.

Democracy: A system where the people enjoy the freedom and will to pursue their own destiny. They are actively involved in the governing process and have the right to vote, criticize and participate in the choosing of leaders, policy and programs.

Democratic Centralism: The unity between freedom and discipline. An organizational system in which policy is decided centrally and is binding on all members.

Dialectics: The study of contradictions within the very essence of things. The art of investigating or discussing the truth of opinions.

Dogmatic: To be rigid and unbending; failing to take into account the changing conditions or the difference between one situation and another.

Economics: The study of social laws governing the production and distribution of the material means of satisfying human needs.

Emotionalism: The practice of acting out of passions, feelings and the spirit of the atmosphere.

Empire: The highest developed stage of a capitalist nation that is characterized by expanding its spheres of influence throughout the world through using military, coup and financial-economic means to gain control over the people and lands.

Ethics: The study of standards of conduct and moral judgment. Deals with ones social relations with comrades, friends, family and associates.

Exploitation: The unjust method of using people for profit and advantage.

Fascism: A repressive form of government that takes on police state characteristics, in that all forms of political, economical and social opposition is forcibly suppressed to maintain the status quo.

Idealism: The concept that states that mind is primary and matter is secondary and that all things originate from the idea and that matter is only a reflection of what exists in the mind, as one perceives it.

Ideology: A system set of principles and beliefs relating to life, culture, politics, etc. Integrated assertions, theories and aims that constitute a socio-political program.

Ideological Struggle: The non-antagonistic, non-physical striving verbally and through practice between different ideologies in trying to prove themselves correct and those opposing incorrect.

Imperialism: The exploitation, rape, and subsequent oppression practiced by one nation over another for greed and profit. The extension of capitalism into the international arena.

Individualism: A narrow selfish approach or outlook based upon putting oneself before the interest of the people, organization, and comrades.

Initiative: The self-reliant exercising of one's imagination, creativity, and the will to tackle all problems, and fervently develop new strategies and programs.

Insurrection: A concentrated attack upon existing authority by members of an oppressed group, usually with the intention of seizing power.

Irresponsible Criticism: Frivolous and irrelevant correcting or pointing out of minor and needless points, which instead of building tears down and obstructs progressive growth and development. The act of criticizing without first investigating and giving the situation thought.

Lackey: A flunky.

Liberation: The state of freedom from a repressive or exploitive existence, where the people have gained control of their lives and have a right to self-determination.

Loyalty: A strong feeling of support and unwavering allegiance.

Lumpen Proletariat: The under class, homeless, unemployed, marginally employed and those who live outside the law.

Mass Line: The political guiding principle of a revolutionary organization that must provide concrete programs for the systematic transformation, stage of the oppressed masses through collective struggles.
Moopie: Movement Groupie.

Neo-Colonialism: Foreign domination of a country or people by imperialist power where the economic, political, and military structure is manned and run by the native petit bourgeoisie. The imperialist maintains control of the economy because they continue to own the means of production, and the client state is totally dependent militarily and politically.

Objectivism: The method of analysis, which takes into account the entirety of the situation. Approaching a situation open-mindedly, wholly and completely without prejudice.

Oppression: Unjust and cruel exercise of authority to deny people human rights.

Petit Bourgeoisie- The middle class or privileged workers, who enjoys a relatively comfortable level of existence, they

167

do not own or control the major means of production, but their main aspiration is to obtain the status, wealth and power of the bourgeoisie.

Policy: The objectives and goals that a group sets for itself along with the means adopted towards the postulated goal.

Politics: A process by which the political and social decisions involving the organization of society are made. The methods of solving contradictions.

Principles: The fundamental grounds on which human beings, organization, movement, cause or concept stands.

Propaganda: The publicized activity by which the party or revolutionary organization politicizes the masses.

Purpose: The reason for doing or being.

Reactionary: Characterized by tendencies toward backward and repressive status quo. Those forces that oppose revolutionary change and actively work to prevent or destroy any progressive movement.

Rebellion: an attack upon existing authority by members or an oppressed group, usually with the intention on the part of the rebels to take state power.

Reformism: The amending and making of internal changes within a system, such as by changing laws, introducing and funding dependency programs without the changing of the oppressive system itself.

Revolt: An organized attempt to seize power without prior organization of the masses in struggle and without any clear set of social objectives.

Revolution: A complete and radical change from one social system into another.

Socialism: A social system in which the people own the means of production and the basis for production is for the people's welfare not profit.

Subjectivism: Injecting one's emotions, passions, feelings in analysis, which results in the narrow one-sided method of drawing situation and all of its relating factors.

Terrorism: The deliberate, systematic, murder, maiming, and menacing of the innocent to inspire fear in order to gain political ends.

Unity-Criticism-Unity: The process of the members of a group, unit or organization united on a set of principles and objectives to struggle internally behind closed doors among themselves by working together, observing and analyzing each others errors and then offering constructive criticism to each other to correct errors and overcome any shortcomings in order to strengthen each other and thus advance the group, unit or organization towards its stated objectives.

Vacillate: To shuck or jive. To waiver from one side to the other.

Vanguard Party: The instrument by means of which the militancy and the rebellion of the revolutionary social forces can be transformed from purely reflexive, trial and error reactions, into purposeful, planned and pragmatic struggles for power.

Acknowledgments:

First and foremost I would like say that ALL praise is due to The Creator of ALL the worlds!

Eternal love to my immediate Ancestors-Sam Pace, Ruth Choice, Anna Brown, Willia Collins, Sarah Bennett, Mama Gaines, Elaine Gaines, Tyrone Gaines and Lorenzo King thank you for all you have shared with me. I will carry you all in my heart as long as I have the ability to.

Love & Respect to Our Revolutionary Ancestors for paving the way and for your continued guidance courtesy of the jewels you left us: Geronimo Ji Jaga, Gil Scott-Herron, Mama Njheri Alghanee, Imari Obadele, Richard Aoki, Marilyn Buck, Mark "Smitty" Smith, "Black Rich", "Big Lady" and all those known an unknown who have affected my path and journey.

To my immediate family: Charles Gaines, Louise Brown, Mary Preston, Freddie Hicks, Margaret King, Nancy Grant, Charlene Baker, Hashim Preston, Jamar Brown, Jonathan Hicks, Inderia Days, Bernie Hicks Melendez, Eboni Joy, Umar Mujahid, Jocquetta Foster, Jarvis Foster, La' Khana Brown, Jeshun Foster, Khaivon Brown, Kheperah-Maat Brown, Tiombe Brown, Kimathi Brown, Kiyomi Brown, Khalesa Brown, Tashmique Younger, Sydney Taylor, Malakai Foster, Malik Foster, Jaevonia Foster, Jesse Cox, Otis Preston, Juan Gaines, John Michael Jones, Gloria Jones and all my countless nieces, nephews, cousins, aunts and uncles that put up with my stubborn, rude Black self. I love you all for life!

To the O.G's (Original Guerrillas): Bilal and Fulani Sunni-Ali, O.G. Shaka At-thinnin, Kumasi, Dhoruba Bin Wahad,

Imam Jamil Al-Amin, Kazi Toure, Ahmad Muhammad, Pam Africa, Mukasa Dada, Kathleen Cleaver, Warrior Woman and the tons of others who have assisted me in being a rebel to Amerikkka! "We will win in spite of ourselves".

To My Warrior Comrades: Balogun and the whole Afrikan Martial Arts Family, Born Divine, Shakmt, Mwalimu and Yaa Baruti, Professor Griff, Marcus Kline, Chairman Fred Hampton Jr., Stic, M1, Immortal Technique, Brother J, Wise Intelligent, Tur Ha, Che, Native Youth Movement, Lina Guerra, Cynthia McKinney and others-Stay on the frontline, Victory is Inevitable.

FTP Family & Supporters: Chosen, Commander Shakur, The Sunni-Ali Family, Mshaniyah, Oluremi, Ajoke, Anew, Flames, Anatea Carpenter, Danielle Kilpatrick, Cedric Head, Serita Fleming, Kiauntay Craig, Myna Lauraine, Lajuanda Moody & Dazeke, Isis Bey, Christine Benjamin, Kevin Baldwin, Warnesa Simmons, Danielle Wright, Taj Anwar, Amond Jackson, Samir & Aja, Ras Kofi, Jaasmeen Hamed, Sadiki Bakari, Shay Ensley, Lorenzo, Biko Kpotufe, Ahjah, Zemiyrah Davis, Jasmine Mitchell, Socks, Derrick & Destiny, Mrs. Bailey, Lia Bennett, Azadeh, Wanjiro, Mike Cheng, Sandra Blaque, Shawnte Payne, Cat, Imhotep Kushan, Janaba Maat, Brother Storm, Miki Vale, The Clean-up Crew, Harmony Rutland, Precise Science, Ka'Ba, Solvivaz Nation, War Club, XPJ7, Karen Mason, Wanique Shabazz, Minister Server, Angie "Hip Hop Angel", Rashida, The Temple of Hip Hop, Afya Ibomu, T.J. Whitaker & The Newark Crew, Jameelah Mullen, Von Proctor, Shawne "H" Bailey, Mister Soul, Goldi Gold, Craig "Flux" Singleton, Vaugnh Saber, Sheree Swann, Shabe, Sister Rah, Eric Ture Muhammad, Bruce George, Ras Marvin, Abdul Muhayman, Abu Jamal, Ubey, West End Community Masjid, William Feagins, Mark & Kiyomi

Rollins, Brother Manifest & HND, Cashawn & Habesha, A. Omar Muhammad, Rabb Love & The Guerrilla Republik Fam, Iz the Truth, The Welfare Poets, Nikijah Haynes, Trig & The Maroon Society, Abundance Child, Kamau Njia, Empress Chi, NYOIL, Iras Levi, Jamahrl "Uno" Crawford, Cisily Elcan, Keza Izm, Kokayi, Naji Mujahid, Emani Bey, Amie Essence, Viva Fidel, Mbaba Hakeem, Makala Fields, Majestic Lovepower, Ain, Damu, staHHr, Arablak, Boog Brown, Quic, Mr. Cool, Zulu Nation/Funk Lordz, Poodie Kinte, Great Scott, Mike Flo, Jaha Asante, Ekundayo, El Sun, Just Black, Thunda, Liuns Den, The DollDaze, Kelly Love Jones, Kelsy Davis, Khalilah Ali, Georgia Me, Nukola, Abyss, Julie Dexter, Killer Mike, Jahi Muhammad, Tahir, Sol Messiah, Sa Roc, Mafdet, Richard Zulu Shabazz, DJ 4th Wurld, La Toya Grant, TaJuana Jones, Lex & Meedy (The Gritty Committee), Ja' Son, J Force, Twice Born, Karin Smoot, Mayasa & Bakari, Mahogany Boisseau, Cardrian Massey, Ebrahim "The Street Journalist", Binta Bin Wahad, Linda Carter, Nisa Shabazz, Chief Kamara, Zayid Malik, Malik Killiam, Big Nel, Taliba, Salakida, Efia Nwanganza, "Godfather" Jihad, Na'imah, Brandi Pettijohn, Kim Roseberry, Carolyn Grady, Dan The Man, Supreme Understanding, Reasun, He-Ruler and the NGE, Yanga, Mr. Gold, Vic & The Othello's Fam, Martina Correia, Troy Davis & Family, Rodney Carmichael, Scienz of Life, Hassan Salaam, Clan Destined, Kil Ripkin, The A-Alikes, J Live, Rita J, the Dubber, Paradise Gray, Jasiri X, Ijahknowah, Vincent Christie, WRFG 89.3, WPKN, Harambee Radio, LIB Radio, The Black August Organizing Committee, MOBB, Mama's Army, Siafu Youth Corps, FTP Catering and all those who have given us a kind word or who support us from near & far- MASSIVE RESPECT for being FOR THE PEOPLE!

To the organizations: International Committee to Support Imam Jamil, African Community Centers For Unity and Self Determination, POCC, Malcolm X Grassroots Movement, NBPP, All African People's Revolutionary Party, UNIA, Uhuru Movement, Nation of Islam –The People depend on us, we all we got…Let's Win! Salute!

FTP Products for Order
http://ftpmovement.ning.com/

Food, Clothes & Shelter: 44 Track
Double Disc Cd $12.99

FTP Movement Anniversary Edition T-
Shirt (Brown/Gold Foil) $20.00

Earrings w/ FTP Logo $10.00

Feed The People Catering Cooking Class
w/ Eboni Joy DVD $10.00

Crew Love T-Shirts $20.00

CPSIA information can be obtained at www.ICGtesting.com
Printed in the USA
LVOW012352150112

263994LV00001B/1/P